WE LESSER
GODS
Addendum

ELIZABETH CLAYTON

Order this book online at www.trafford.com
or email orders@trafford.com

Most Trafford titles are also available at major online book retailers.

Print information available on the last page.

ISBN: 978-1-4907-7542-5 (sc)
ISBN: 978-1-4907-7544-9 (hc)
ISBN: 978-1-4907-7543-2 (e)

Library of Congress Control Number: 2016911784

Trafford rev.   07/21/2016

Trafford
PUBLISHING®   www.trafford.com
North America & international
toll-free: 1 888 232 4444 (USA & Canada)
fax: 812 355 4082

Introduction

Introductory remarks to this small piece,
"Addendum to 'We Lesser Gods'."
need be only brief and exclusively explanatory.
Most of that needed said is included
in the "Pefacing Addendum" to the primary work, itself,
"We Lesser Gods."
However, perhaps good reasoning might be
to express just why it is present.
It merely serves to indicate that there was a year of great
transitional verse before "We Lesser Gods" was brought
together. It was an unconscious struggle, and I did not recognize
the exercise of the matter, laying aside the verses
toward which I did not feel comfortable.
The "Addendum" is a transitional piece, at least to me, in
retrospect, a missive which, after dissonance
about the verses, and their
being put aside, I reviewed sometime later,
with several re-readings, and
I came to find the dissonance, the coming
to surface, doubt and despair,
but a good deal of other worthy material, also. --
not to lose the melody of "one falling petal,"
I am now including all of my ruminations
concerning faith, doubt -- wishing
to clasp its entire essence, the year 2013 included.
I found, with a great deal of humility, that existence is greater
than any one record of it that we can make.

Some "lighter" pieces are included since I am
not always dark, as surely others, also;
I am cognizant of the principle that existence
involves, realistically, the inclusion
of the joy of the feast -- all is simply steps in the dusts of time
toward completeness and peace.
Behind, then, are all of my verses of 2013, with a
small smattering of others as a reprieve for the
personal struggle -- aware, and in great
part, unaware -- during that year.
Perhaps "readiness"" stages are realities.

-- in the afternoon, better for some respite from delving into
the heavy and discordant -- if, often, without resolution --

Elizabeth
March 14, 2016
just at daybreak

A Verse Confessional

I am unfamiliar with myself tonight,
the hours moving into their earliest morning time,
and I look closely to my own feelings, sentiments left of a day.
And I feel away from whoever I most think I am –
not quite at ease, more, at great unease.
Christmas is near, and such time marks many visits to
the plains of Carthage,
the intensity of all losses of the fabled Dido, and
words, somehow, now, inappropriate, of the
grande secretary's words, on leaving his post.
Perhaps quiet and still, the winds in gusts of frigid air in
the outdoors – perhaps these appointments
arranging around this late hour dutifully call out
reflection, an often
evaluative exercise, leaving a balance, waiting, a stance
not unkind to my accepted self.
But most bears a challenge, an exclamation of my
knowing self that appears with skewed qualities, and
in that quality, irredeemable.
Stubbornly, I hold these elements to myself,
philosophically documenting, exacting their colors most
pleasing, falling into a kind of elderman of
compassionate stance.
Andso, I am, and I am not, as to where the world's glory
begins; but with a small sadness, I choose to,
in the moment, hold to the self, away from myself, it as a
truer self, if alone, and in quickly passing appraisals,
less than acceptable.
But, in the choosing, is a contentment; I will wait
full morning to reassess, knowing that part of the
exercise will have become a new part of me,
refreshing, and more complete.

Elizabeth
in deepest night
December 15, 2013 – true anniversary to Richard's
death in 1992 – now twenty-one years –
– too much of "me," and sleep would ease my dissonance, but then
sleep is such a waste, intellectually – or otherwise –
– I think, a different contentment – I really do not know –

a "sweet piece, as per Jonah, I would think; but
such is comforting to my ever angst -

-a sweet pain into peace -
knowing to banish the thought;
tears giving over a smile of resignation -

We do not let the thought go all the way out because we
cannot fully embrace – such is the protection of the self -

I know only that I live, truly, in the "shadow of
death" - in each moment, of all my days -

And these moments, rare, when we are not aware, we
are losing, losing on the feet of each moment's passing,
into that great void where death continually reigns -

But still, my parents' will: I believe that I will live,
and I will know into contentment, and the fires of my
passion will leap their fullest, their most true -

an elizabeth afterthought:
coming throughout the day -

Elizabeth's Pentangle
Five Cantos

And in the tomorrow, who will find love to me –
for in my thought I hear the ancient
lament: "It is, again, cold, and I am, again, alone."
Sentimental wanderings find love in yesterday,
my amber ones, reminding, in the
hours of seasonal change, and fulfilling:
from their tender strengths, the faces of
my needing self can, in
contemplation's quest, find conclusion with content.
Yet, in the increasing years, when I was
still raven, my sport was in playing passion
with reason, the marriage of these progressing toward truth.
However, they, others and I, could
not bide the hours, the entire becoming
a task, of giving rather than the gift of reciprocity,
in the matter of devotion.

Andso, in the tomorrow, who will find love to me –
visitations, of all varieties, have brought the
marvel of dreams – known beauty, in its growth into
the phenomenon of change, staying its
companion, lovely constancy:
the glory of first light – its flowing out into finding;
the diminutive small in splendid rounds of Chrysanthemum
radiance; dew fall sparkling, and refreshing
winds offering chilled leaves, falling, blowing
summer's patient husbandry, a palette into
autumn's wealthy countenance.
Whisperings, and falling sighs – piercing into their deep – these,
humanity's truest gold; in a very deluge
of memory, the growing fragrance of wood fires touch
hands and heart.

A love, then, will find, in the lighted first of being,
in place, and in thought – in every hour
of the closeted knowings with
the procession of time. And in today's tomorrow,
in every day's tomorrow, love will find to me in all –
if in loneliness, and grief -- of what has been -- or what can
never be – but golden is acceptance, if embellished
about in the wealthy robes of
recognition, and the realization of the must
rearranging
of passion, these in deliverance toward quiet
and gently known content.
Beautiful, then, is to visit at table,
to, in narratives, sweet, know the troth, past
description, of thought and sentiment, in which the days
of the sunken pomegranate's cheeks are worded into coming to be;
a joining saga, a metamorphose in that of delicious, adventuresome
rebellion, these into tears, and Samaritan bindings out the
armored heart; advancing, still, philosophical joustings come
to smile at doubt and questioning, into a meadow of
stillness, dressed in silence, these varietal
principles coming to be put aside,
not in denial or impotence, but
in truth of mortal unveiling, a final crown to
us "lesser gods."

Then, oh then – a balance strikes, the heart becoming tender
in its constricted heaviness. This magic lies in
every morning, the hours flowing love, if
individually experienced. The fuller histoire finds all –
the thief, the leper, the courtesan; the savior, kings and
serfs, yet the cynic, the cleric, and the warrior.

− Tomorrow − the clock is still, to reason, the attire
of the players in full fluidity. And the
movement is all of time.
There is no anemic answer, to her consort, the
unfounded question; the wine and the grape
are one; all is in the moment's flow, and, in the
moment, is all of time.

Elizabeth
two forty-five am
November 5, 2013

thoughts, deep into the night, each leading
to fundamental constructs
in the understanding of the grey, and sometimes bright
"openings," in the path (roads) of life. The conclusion
is one being worked toward, out great
dissonance − fire and passion, of necessity, of examination, full.
I can know, with the breathlessness of Dante
under his stars, to finally accept that given,
except the fashioning of my stance chosen, in it.
Harpies are still realities to us mortals,
but grief prepares content, and,
then, there is the "balance," of "walking these golden,
earthly sands."

− "Walking these … earthly sands." − the refrain
for a verse to my mother, my child,
my sister, my friend − years ago on "Mother's
Day," following her death −

A construct referring to the armor of "Sir Gawain and the
Green Knight" is the reference for the title of this verse; the
piece was written by an old English poet
known as "the Pearl Poet."
Sir Gawain's armor was decorated with a red, five-pointed star
representing the complete (good) knight (man).

The "openings" and (roads) of life written
into this verse refer to often
used words and phrases from the work of the modern, American
poet, Robert Frost.

The "stars of Dante" phrase can be referenced back to his grande,
Medieval work, "The Divine Comedy," part, "The Inferno;"
Stars, in all of Dante's works represent God's presence and love.

— —

Statements Quartre

Friends are lid snippets of gold dancing upon a meadow's dew fall;
kin is like wealth in the hymnody
learned though innocence,
in early faith;
greatest beauty found in casting about
is in the countenance of Holy Presence,
spreaded out through woodlands, free,
rivers, flowing, mountains, in very being.
All is simplicity, woven into the moment,
when good is the seeking, almost similar,
but quickly departing the familiar,
if wandering into a venture of the ungood.
These statements quartre, appear as an
exercise of running in place:
nowhere in beginning, nowhere in concluding –
a pleasant jingle to recite –
Yet, they are, in truth, expressions of the idiot's wisdom,
the child's finesse, the monarch's tortuous despair;
these knowings make rainbows, and sighs – and laughter, the
gentle paisley pattern, its endless beginnings and endings –
they become images of emulation for comfort in our strength,
the freshest joy in our expectations.

November 20, 2013
two o'clock am

–enjoying reviewing the wisdoms in the art of
living well – revenge – or an annunciation!

Blessed Beginnings

And I slept into the first night,
within its premier light,
near the dreamer's flowing stream,
the quiet turtle, beside.
I heard the silence of centuries past,
punctuated by invited murmurings
of the maiden day.
And into this prelude, I felt new tension, to enter,
a pleasing dissonance, that of unkempt warmth,
as passion in first love,
and all the excitings, the properties, thereof –
...and I slept into the first night, to, bye the bye,
know blessed beginnings,
the very joy of the feast of life –

upon rising, in gentle rainfall
January 1, 2013
spontaneous words, in first darkness, but fully
cognizant of every raindrop –

Achieving the Pentangel

I must not – with extremes of effort, yet, more –
cannot come to die, to, better, please,
drift through mists, the inaudible sweetness of goodbyes,
and sighings – through tears, the emerging
surmise of eternal beauty –
lest I free my poor, my beggar soul –
of darkness, – a covered smallness; including, still,
deceitful manipulation, and the scourge of betrayal--
the most heinous of evil.
My complextion must come to be bronzed of honor
held into, and kept, my strength of,
and terror to, harm such as the gladiators,
instructed of Satan's will;
my lips must form smiles that remind, only, the cold,
in waiting seed, the crimson apple's round,
the throat of the exquisite, early Lily.
Straw feathers of the green-flamed bamboo,
together with its handsome joints,
and the drifting about of grey smoke -
lost, left over coal -
these images must find a warm hearth in my inner knowings,
though windborne to my reason.
We cannot be the good we know, or wish,
but, in its surrounding thought we will
soften more to its carrying messages –
truth, reason – with the knight of fullest love who beds
with its sentiment, press me, award my understanding,
leave me with the shield of the pentangel in red.

July 13, 2015
afternoon

a confusion of gender, but a blend of the egalitarian qualities,
those described in the old, Medieval piece, *Sir Gawain and
the Green Knight, the design engraved on his shield of red color –
signifying the five points of complete good; this piece is attributed
to the ancient writer called the "Pearl Poet" (unknown)* – this,
my piece, appears hurried in finishing, and will need more
work, toward a slow, more concluding sentiment –

The Generosity

The generosity in solitude offers such gifts
as those suggesting a pause, yet, then, a bow,
to the presence of afforded thought –
for in light and dark, constructions come to form
a rare beauty –
the very nearness of the elusive self.
Quickly, as the dawn breaks, or dew fall exudes
its first freshness, comes a clasping,
an opening of a door, the mirror –
the vocabulary which announces the reality of
very personal identity: a flowing length of rare silk,
brought by crusades' blood, it to become embroidered of
select stones whose light and fire remind the rainbow –
together with stitched, pressed flowers,
those whose captured smiles, appear as first,
recognizing the small and grande;
yet, the mundane against rich complexity, to laugh
into a rainfall of cascading green apples –
self in light – in early morning hours,
a cloth laid out of gifts which had only been seen
before in uncomfortable dissonance,
together with disquieting announcement of truest need.
Time with awareness, senses and thought,
and attention to the physical self, provide a literature to be gently,
if purposefully, taken up through hours -
the personal holding of the flowing silk,
loosening stones, beautifully prophetic,
and dreaming of the once lovely radiance
of quieted hours painted into the ambiance
of pressed blossoms, their hues as variegated wines.

Time, time – soften the hours, for I have drunk deeply
yours provided aperitif, its purity in advance of its passion,
to then burn the raging fire, waiting.
This such of mine has been taken by your pirating winds –
give back, give back – touch warmest kisses
to my sunken breasts, and write, once again,
an histoire of the filled stem, over and again, it red of blood,
with heat of flame, a touching of the very
superlative sensing in being.

The Leften

If there be now only the true leften,
then I will not to fall into impotent loss,
but rise, if with misgivings beside whole pondering,
to embrace the two paths
of the finished leften:
these – to take the residue, and immortalize
its spreaded, if lost glory;
or to go beyond its left absence, its emptiness,
its, perhaps, unseen, fallow beauty;
and when I am in the dark pasture of the absence,
I will find, in my paled dreams, within the folds of my garments -
annointings, spirit, wisdom -
and a portion of kept beauty – yet, not at all representative,
of its source.
But found will be a relic whose likeness is that of the seed,
it to die, yet to fall, in its immediacy,
into waiting soil – that of which I will water with my
lamentations, enrich with my wanting care--
to bring it again to a full beauty –
as the rare camellia, in winter's chill, but with spring's
giving promise; to offer a pleasing, a yet superlative gift,
one of fullest pleasant hue, form exemplary,
and most, in manifest, an exquisite undersided
colour of a slightest, glowing crimson.

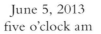

June 5, 2013
five o'clock am

On a decision of quite great import, following days, months –
drawing out, and returning, learning from memory,
even into fatigue; projecting into what days there are,
indeed have always been: the leften, and a decision, finally,
to give into the river which continues,
not ever, yet, pausing, to flow –

And the unkind fate of that which is, and its
playing out – the pressed weltanschaunng –
we are merely mournings to the plan already in place – and yet,
the "lions" to be seen – on the "...beach in the moonlight."
Hemingway, *The Old Man and the Sea*

Early Image, One

White gold in morning

A blaze of white gold,
abbreviated glory -
yesterday – brought within its center;

I wish all of it,
for it is all of me –

An ambiance of self,
with no castings off –
ever beautiful, all grace, manifest,
Amen.

February 16, 2013
Thoughts at full sunrise, from my bedroom –

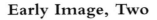

Early Image, Two

White gold in the morning

Again today,
the morning's most first complete:
it appeared more rounded than a sweeping wash,
but I could not look into its
intense whole,
only to know the glory it brought –
the ambiance of great and humble –
the sweet assurance of provided grace.

February 18, 2013
near eight o'clock am
morning's first – full sunrise, to my awareness
from my bedroom window

Besting the Living Perishing

When pain and longing
come to shared presence,
in their fullness and their emptiness,
weep, weep the hour,
for the universal of all importances diminishes,
almost as wind in a brief farewelling,
or, knowing the reality of flowing water.
Nothing else is in presence nor is cognizance of any other
approachable construct:
love, the unacceptably tender, perhaps;
transgressions, of now, only with some import;
and Christmas, come the tired fable.
Can the spirit of us "lesser gods" best this impotence,
this living perishing —
circumstance and will, together, decide.

December 24, 2013
near midnight
— some unkind visitations, including unhappy depersonalization

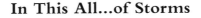

In This All...of Storms

The full flight is come,
and the unbelievable is caught –
my thought cannot
process to its full knowing,
only to drink from the cup, beginning.
Voices from within manifest
in small realities, and call out demons
that kill my reason and resolve.
The "fields of glory" dance among the voices
and I cannot see their colors well;
perhaps they feel my fullest angst,
more powerful than the sun who calls
out their smiles and promises,
and attending angels.
Silent, silent the familiar bells, who speak,
now, these years, to full attention –
lost, lost – it all to nothing, nothing in all,
the lostness now, ever.
Steps, steps – these will come for me,
in this all of Lear's mountainous storms.

August 7, 2013
eleven-twenty pm

Two

Words and words of sound, and in silent tumult,
fears within my own;
how to escape, and with whom to go –
no one, none and – quiet;
blessed is the simple quiet
the humbled sent to his quiet feast.

-in deepest night

My True
Three

Let the beautiful, my true –
these to die with me,
all before I die.
Let my thought, in that scripted,
and all executed, each with my hand,
find pleasure, to do, yet,
let these find cloister in hearts,
akin, and those select, of all that
universe of the thoughtfully felt.

August 7, 2013
in deepest night

of my pieces, each in a moment of accounting, after
the episode of great hallucinations,
fearful of loss of emotional and cognitive abilities –

Elizabeth Thoughts
Four

Out the failing blossom
finds the sweetest breath
to give, then, from;
the forgotten, gifted music box,
its melody, in near travail,
but of truest love, telling;
our hearts in reflection bring
the spent of sentiment to wound,
over, most, poignantly, again.

In the Lone...

In the lone of night
I saw a door,
brightest halo of purist light,
fair truth, all around —
and I said,
"Should it be opened."

August 10, 2013
in deepest night

Shadows Five

Shadows are gathering just outside reflection,
cameos of the past "now,"
and echoes followed by softened sighs.
With these, very chariots of valued steps,
gold, enough, not having been kept,
that warmth be, in greatest need.
Com back, these golden steps,
the paths of mingled joy and weeping,
instruction, beyond its bearing;
but in it, bringing the gold for fading whispers,
making, fast, the lock that stores love and faith –
with a portion of strength.
The way home is the long way,
keeping passion beside its resting.
The radiance of new thought will sit
close inside those who hold, out,
the baton to hands of all keepers
of order and spontaneity, building the good,
in dark of hearts
which carry the beauty of gold;
the interior face, its noble visage, lost to gifts of treasure,
that must – yet, its thought relayed,
redeeming all before, the leften settling down
as dust, of years carrying the beginning of again.

August 10, 2013
in deepest night

Thanksgiving Eve, 2013

Halleluiah, Alleluia, all praise and honor to Thee,
oh God –
for Thou hadst wakened me from
another "little death,"
to live in joy out certain dark.
Forgive and bless,
and in the all of plenty,
accept true praise, and gratefulness.
The hearth Thou saw to take from us,
but we, in days of wisdom, granted,
live, yet, in gratitude and adoration.
Amen.

First Thoughts

I do not wish ought, in these hours
of old Chanticleer –
to either ready my steps, if as purposed
with my cane,
or to sound my voice,
it beside the sentiment of my only heart;
for there is none to whose eye my spirit flames,
leaping with joy,
nor any still, more,
whose hands ache for my hungry touch.
O God – if everlasting Thou surely be,
close forever this yearning in emptiness.

January 17, 2013
four-thirty am
first thoughts

To Our Departed Gold

The falling of a warrior, the concluding of a year's days,
yet the lessening of the lovely petal –
or when a day has wandered into its twilight hour –
an expression, a commemorative word,
need be voiced, perhaps, and surely, many.
We cannot keep ought that we hold,
whether we love or no –
but there are avenues down which we
may walk that offer benedictions, ever living,
to our departed gold.
Feast or hanging shield, darkest dirge,
yet softened candle flame –
a pilgrimage or a signatured missive –
perhaps a portioned silence, an escaping sigh –
these, then, stand out the heart's larder,
full with words in varying manifest,
that we have lived and died the day,
it to be rainbowed, echoing – carried forward,
as resting in the constancy of the seasons,
perpetual.

January 28, 2013
in deepest night

The Releasing

The winds of time blow ever,
ever, always, passing their hewning force
through our days; as the wheel and hand,
move and shape, casting away,
such moments of lifting dew;
and blossoms are left to fashion –just so–
at the taking away of the lovely effervescence.
Quietly these energies smile on their
spectacular activity, patterning a fire,
raging into flamed amens – when we are all, somehow,
cognizant in recognizing this beautifully
appointed model.
A mourning accompanies the recognition,
the passing of winds, of dew, and the marvelous
shaping of that they wish.
And we "wretches" who grieve the select,
this rare ceremony, do not rend or froth,
but rather find a companionable stream by which to sit,
and ponder, to then marvel the munificence of all good,
and rise to finish waiting, blessed work,
to grow more into the feast –
to find joy and peace in the very nature of being –
its press, absolute:
Mississippi, gifted summer rain, all time –
every movement finds a releasing of spirit to the openness–
that and spontaneity within generous soul.

July 27, 2013
three-fifteen am

Fallen Daylight

Eleven fifteen, or there near to – closing, soon,
now the day, but, truly, an hour – properly -
of sad farewells – for more, much more -
is lost, quickly lost – into the away,
into an eternity that is know, most,
a matter of semantics, they resting somewhere within us
where words are merely topical -
and inside our day, but must to bear a heavy dark.
And sleep – it does restore,
but it maneuvers a great loss, yet, still -
a match, a candle, a flame or lamp,
perhaps the moon, floating in soft, gray heavens -
I wish to never sleep, that all time be of daylight,
nor be grandmother to any,
however the crowns they offer, but, again,
with loss, noted and ledgered.
Ah, in sweet fatigue I perish myself, to fall,
certainly, to the full carat,
the established pedigree,
the kindly necessity of moments of unawareness -
oblivion – if appointed by some mystical phenomenon
of pleasant dreams, our full selves burked,
through the wisdom of Morpheus.

March 9, 2013
near midnight

DST coming in, andso within, "correctly,"
the first hour of new day -

a not, (verse), possibly describing, gently,
my ever mania – demonstrably, in long, recent days -

The Hawk's Cry

In the hawk's cry, through matins sung
within birds' callings;
in fruit giving to the day;
in the silent noise of my soul,
we are all as one, a helpless flow,
the carrying out of our voices' mourning,
still other lamentations,
heard against the distant glow of the rising.
And we, as only more, within the hands of nothing,
become, as all, together, beautiful,
illusive nothing, with such comfort, only,
of the morning laughter in coming farewelling,
but, fated, yet, to wander the eternal night of time past.

Early morning, before rising –

— a fragment found in an side folder, written in deep of night,
under heavy medication, but rousing to an image,
its meaning, now, not completely understood other than the
veil of dark mourning –

This is a masterful drawing of my statement
then, and most of now.
Interestingly, to me, the hawk was especially admired
by Richard, for its absolute freedom,
and, I think, its qualities of the masculine, both of which
Richard felt imprisoned in their loss to his real self.
I have written one other verse of the hawk, and Richard –
their deaths — and the nobility of them.

These latter statements were written in the spring and fall of 2013,
when found again, in reviewing older work;
the verse was written August 2, 2001; I have rewritten the verse,
somewhat, because of what appears to me, now,
as "poor writing," - errors – in mechanics,
not in the sentiment expressed –

A Grief Observed

Relationship with time is most requiring,
that it is, in reality, only
moments, and they, in their realities,
only passings into farewelling.
They make their presence in their chiding,
in faint remembrance,
in the hurting knowing of lostness, and its softened
criticism of our somewhat adolescent unawareness.
Perhaps most painful is our penchant for conjuring up
the substance of that lost, moments of
patience's ease, echoes of worded sonnets,
full with descriptive, intense oneness – of beauty
in all of its guises: of verity, the hidden necessities
of our hearts, those to be known, only, in this fashion –
a glimpse, apart, of who we are, through
our shadowed needs, the essence of our souls' pressing,
known ever, only, in its lovely,
westward dim.

Elizabeth
in deepest night
(– morning, near five o'clock)
November 30, 2013

– thoughtful of recent, past scapes – relating,
and resting/resignation in it all –

The title of this verse can be referenced back to a work
by the same title, by C. S. Lewis, recounting
his grief following his wife's death; it was given to
me by one of my second husband's roommates from
college; my marriage to Richard lasted almost twenty-
three years, that of Lewis, only a year or so.
The unfortunate comparison of the two marriages
shows that Lewis grieved from loss of a
beautiful relationship, which could not be replaced,
mine a loss of the opportunity to bind a
most unhappy marriage, one, with Richard's death, truly not ever,
that could not be made whole. However, beauty, in any fashion,
if lost, is subject for grief, and the theme for this piece was
initiated by the season, Richard's death occurring
on December 15, twenty-one years ago.

The Arranging

Night hours arrange slowly, silently,
in impotent stances, and one's thought is a devoted companion,
if courtesan to appetites which offer new paths,
those which spar with magic and sensation,
the imbibing of bliss in protective solitude.
To be alone is to look freshly toward new ideas,
sentiments — the avenues and boulevards sponsoring
angst and fear — all to be dressed by the courtesan's
suggestions, more, her willed intentions.
To be alone is to sit, the janused hearth god,
perishing beside a struggling birth,
and in the full of it, is the turn that is feared, yet embraced -
passion's warmth to be caught in the salad
of circumstance offered -
a wager of the proportions of a quest -
out a slumber can come resolve and purpose -
what then but to salute, for the moment -
for many, may, yet, be granted in life of the desert
with no response, suddenly teased into purposed thought -
movement was — yes — a balance, struck — trying,
in absolute impoverishment — trying, else to perish.
I am not caught, yet, "in springtime's fields of glory" -
not yet — blood of soul — balm to must to sleep -

January 20, 2013
four-thirty am

wretched struggle — the crumpled handkerchief

composed in deepest night, with some unclear
sentiments, upon waking, to transcribe -

"Knighting" the "Lesser Gods"

Knowing truth is descriptive of finding place
in diffused light, and it, filled,
to be separated with shade and vapors –
often, sunlight and clear, may be as much,
the lady making her countenance,
colors added, to be softened, and, then,
to be taken away;
but if time is allowed, the day's steps, "will out" –
"it" always does –
the sainted troth, in springtime, sometime,
almost, often, is achieved, the knighting of we,
the "lesser gods."
The face, sponsoring the features, the will,
pushes forth, and we meet to clasp, and hold, to know
our absolute press toward the mark,
we waiting seekers, to find the postulate
of the wager, a fashioned visage,
rose and ivory, dressing Romanesque leanings –
our treasure, a satisfied whole, the complete,
of the appointed care,
an accepted knowing.

August 12, 2013
an exercise, in bed, upon awakening – my notes are unclear,
and incomplete – just a guess at transcribing -

sleep, a strumpet, as a tease, to hold out its comings -

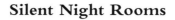

Silent Night Rooms

In the silent rooms of night,
rehearsals are concluded, costumes put aside,
and lines become almost a wonder,
their prompting not ever in place.
For within the night, levels of thought, the "reasonable"
of the day light's stage, are somehow lost,
to full awareness, cognition in its most, clear rendering.
The raw self, in innocence's clothing,
takes the stage with an impromptu speech –
a soliloquy – a soliloquy whose lines are all more memorable than
those of the highborne tragic, those, now,
of humanity's current spokesman.
In the silent rooms of night, a confession is sweet,
anger is spent, into a nebulous,
untouchable dankness, and love is,
in worded description, found;
the fear of loss, of the construct of season –
age, dependency, death –
such as these are brought out for
acknowledgment, and recognition,
bound to the existential in the mundanely,
conscious aware;
the unexpressed hunger for power, esteem, position,
even in that of poor estate – piety visited,
the superlative "casual" - these stripes emerge quiet the true,
in the silent rooms of night,
through natural law and condition of will.

And we writhe, as the Mariner's beautiful water snakes,
filled of truths we may hardly bear,
to quickly out into the heaviness of a world in light,
that our behaviors and thought,
arrange in docile, rose tones,
spun out the poet's line of... "revenge... in living well."
Leviathan, now again, awareness, inside,
lies, a forced sleep,
to raise its heavy prison in another,
troubled room of night.

May 9, 2013
in deepest night

Mostly Unclear Images

The beauty in light is as the sacredness of all good;
light steps away the innocent moments of our day.
We are halos and echoes,
born with heaviness –
Spills and water –
If joy can be of differences,
lace and satin against whiteness our goal –
pretty–

late summer, 2013
in deepest night – as sleep was taking –

I lay upon my friendly companion,
it in knowing of the complexities of my thought:
each earlier path, the struggle in past ventures,
the excitement in the whole of my eye;
this moment will arrive into history 'round an ambiance,
convenient – present, calling to expression of the closeting,
probably because of a part of my histoire,
either in\of my histoire –
and now – this moment, I, unencumbered
by will or circumstance –
I speak!

late summer, 2013
written late at night when I was close to
another level of consciousness –
not able to read well–
but, to me, a mostly clear fragment

This Continuing

When I lie in the shadowed portion of the day,
moreso, seemingly, when the season of spring
is giving over to that of summer –
in company of my thought, alone, to itself –
the silence comes to sing, a lullaby of long ago,
and far away;
and the softening light falls, a gentle smile,
as close as the always far away.
Recollection courts my thought, from many gardens,
fields, and glens, together with roads
which lead into quite, many gatherings –
in these such moments, reminders fill my dreams,
awake, into fancy:
as, when the vapors are kind –
roses, clusters, here and there,
fragrant and rare, without flaw or blemish,
unless in presence of an early dewdrop,
or the sun's, yet bathing, golden rays.
Everything in this fore is past record,
appearing near, in the certain of its distance:
characters, realities, all, sentiments,
yet truths in their dress of the clever abstract –
never to be, but always, somehow –
without sadness, as in great passion –
to not ever clasp again.

And then, the hour is almost the encompassing dark,
the memories, a lost loveliness,
a mirror of that of all good;
I rise to chart my steps into the magic,
the mystery of night –
empty and filled, together, with
the question of many occasions – into which my
thought crashes, so that I stagger, nearly to fall –
but not yet, not yet:
what then, of this continuing.

April 8, 2013
begun in eventide, the close of a difficult,
but rewarding day; transcription completed near ten o'clock pm
"as it came" –

And Let Me Walk...

And let me walk in the royalty of sunlight,
from the kingship of all good –
with every rising, bathed in mists of morning dew,
in queenly fashion of premier greens –
not any dim of backward turnings;
no angstful pondering in forward thirstings,
only the gold in each covering
of all intrusive thought;
let gratitude fall from first awareness,
together with the whole of day,
and come, may be, a quiet lying down that,
finally, the every animal has its place,
and the monarch, in his robe of color,
surveying all about the bejeweled straw;
and trees, with their own magnificat,
may, under twilight's growing moon –
may be – to wind their way, together with the very earth,
in flesh of generous centuries, supporting,
blessing every conclusive thought.

on rising, enjoying breakfast, prelude to a portion
of accepted grace –
a small prayer\statement

summer's radiance,
bowing to the autumn smile – oh please –

brief wisdom verses from 2013

Out Fullest Divinity

Let me, now, and let me, please,
hold the rope of hope in prayer to Thee,
Thy listening heart, Thy generous giving.
The world, created in beautywealth, nods too often –
that I am without recourse,
save Thee Whose vigilant omniscience knows
the uneven balance as it moves between
the created concrete, and the created spiritual.
This dissonance leaves me dependent on the one constant,
the truest true on which
to lay the wage with the day.
Grant, please, that not the jaundiced eye,
devoid of joy in lack, with wanting, make the wait,
but with lack, without, objective purity out Thy intercession
with my heart.
Let come a peace that moves in grace and faithful constancy,
that I may rise, my joy renewed, not liturgy,
nostalgic sentiment, complexions, fair –
or observations, curious, but of the forward appendage
of thought – hope,
from the bowels of mercies being drawn
out full divinity.

May 21, 2015
in a desperate moment – mid-morning

Waking...

The silence into which I wakened, suddenly,
possibly from sounds foreign to
some level of consciousness,
whose ear was sensitive, sounds threatening –
outside, or within my rooms –
this silence was not silent, but an inundation,
a deluge of bells, my, now, familiar "sandgrains"
all falling, but not ever reaching their fall,
simultaneously – so that a fluidity effected,
almost to distraction, in intensity,
within my uncomposed, waking self.
My scalp became constricted, for as I drew my parameters,
– no help found – the hour, earlier than I wished,
– not near, yet, daybreak, and only an occasional sound
– of wheels that sponsored life – others –
– perhaps to offer solace,
– if press required.
Comin, the seventh day,
Sabbath, and the lie I keep,
to be spent with necessities, taxes and such –
getting toward late February –
but not with hymns and prayers other than those rising
spontaneously from great need – without liturgy,
except that of the abiding Natural.
The chocolates, perhaps opened in the day,
and now put away, left over from the celebration
of the young – hearts and flowers – these, concepted,
lay like old crumbs, near my bed, against "elizabeth" gifts.

Cognizant of the whole of nothing, my poor leg, as now,
constant – I feared for my reason, must to catch a bark,
some bark within my chilled rooms, the heat anemic,
having been repaired in nearby days;
unrecognizable sounds continued,
at times punctuating the bells,
and my thought became more
incompatible to my sentiment,
searching – I thought I heard my geese in the south woods,
just briefly, and their nonsensical voices brought true tears;
confused, I referenced to a short verse written hurriedly
in the early coming day, just yesterday,
the blaze of white gold, the triumph over another dark,
lone journey: the great triumph – I again lived,
and if mercurial, well.

February 17, 2013
on waking, in deepest night
Greg's birthday, and he does not know,
often, or at all, that I exist –
or that I remember the first hours, days of his life –

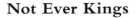

Not Ever Kings

I turned to the day, without any awareness,
only direction toward my purposed thought –
passing, merely hours, and – caught –
between the cruel past and the cruel moment's tomorrow –
The mind appears – with a "however" insisting –
always, to protect itself,
finding apartments which arrange its thought,
possible for lengthy hours.

– andso –

Does a kind of wealth lie to the side of stored thought,
yet that of pain,
and the loss of gentle hope –
perhaps we walk bravely when we are directed
by threatening sponsors of the day,
that we not falter in our steps.
One continues, then, into the night, and darkness covers
all strength that has been walked upon;
the seams of our compartments begin to ravel,
and ebb, so that awareness attacks what is,
with the froth of clarity and truth.
Ought left is to quieten today's lamps,
and to remember and weep,
to forgive and hope.

We live in a poorly constructed riddle which catches light
in an idle moment, from distant worlds,
to offer, in just such beautiful moments,
splendor and glory;
and sometimes we can wear crowns,
but we can not ever be kings.

March 19, 2013
late, the day after beginning "battling down–"

Reflections

After bathing, I returned to bed, the hour arriving
to only the morning's two o'clock,
since I had awakened.
The clock was in its journey; I heard the night sounds,
cries of night animals – in birthing,
feeding, with primitive soundings of need I could not
understand – and added were the small voices
rising, tenuously, from within my secret self.
I felt, as I had in the day, passed, a quiet sabbath,
very aware, and somewhat, then, lonely, but most,
content, if with alertness, to constant observation.
Presently, the small voices of self–competed with the
voices of solitude, my familiar "bells, the locusts'
drones of my childhood in long, unbroken –
troubled – if beautiful summer days,
days which wandered, uninhibited,
into the waiting, the vastness of quiet eternity.
The present voices spoke of the seasons,
their sentiments of conclusion, of new beginnings:
changes, fears, including inconsistencies,
betrayal, illness, untruthfulness in many complextions –
and certain loss.
The animal cries began to soften and die into the night
into the far darkness, as I had allowed to do with my silent voices;
the chill of winter is only a persona we must acknowledge,
for it is preparing new beginnings,
with our will and hope which culminates
in the radiance of summer;
we lose with every step, forward, the unhappy,
but truly sweet pain of all that ever was,
that we in the springs, our winters –
harvest, which, like a leaping flame of gold,
signatures the unspeakable, passionate radiance of summer.

Memory is long and painful, and giving
— so left the wisdom of present
voices: andso, I lighted a candle of vanilla fragrance,
and thought, with a kind of peace, of young women,
in faraway yesteryear, who, in waiting their Christmas guests,
pinched their lips and cheeks for rose, and visited
their pantry for a sweet flavoring to be placed behind the ear –
promise! In the door to open –

Content, with Difficulty

Difficulty weaves all about individuality,
and the concept of silence, emptiness, outside,
and different share their descriptive features.
The result, in many instances, is cruelty,
whether of insecurity, idle thought,
or arranged schedules that do not allow concern.
Beauty is in all things – however the quiet, the empty,
the outside, the different – to offer up very bouquets of loveliness
to the individual within these spheres;
music so made, flowers cultivated, likeso, can be brought
to their particular rarities – metaphorically
or in objective reality -
these only portend the glory of a soul when
pressed in his own individual fashion.
Glory finds in the shroud that this person dons,
and it is his statement to his fellows -
although they cannot ever know
the richness of the self within -
the present cleanliness of spirit,
the achievement of independent thought,
and the intense praise in knowing
of a day of life, aware, content.

March 22, 2013
assessing, at two o'clock am

alone, but not lonely, empty of much, full with more;
content, with nothing, but satisfyingly full, of all -

the construct of "singlehood" has been in my thought,
these present, past days -

Morning, Again, Came In!

Ah, glory abundance: halleluiahs rising upward, again,
the tomb, empty and silent, more, the prodigal, returned –
and the morning, again, came in!
In natural splendor, these kept all, in ambiance:
geese sounding in the south woods;
the etching in of golden brilliance, emitting other,
which glow in alleluia hues,
time somehow now giving over to more review,
and a slowness positioned in a kind of elegance and grace.
With the passion of a very lover, a quietness lingers –
a stillness lies about – the exciting passing of shadow,
the dying wind; the knowing of a presence of contentment
in acceptance of the day past,
that just stepped through.
Hear, hear the magnificent! And then, the familiar exuberance,
the promise; the thrust toward an expression out oneself –
yet reaching out of the self –
for the divine through beauty's coming reality,
out true, elemental fire; a moment of thought
comes into its own, with anticipation growing out of physical
elements, the tender hewning of sentiment,
yet the phenomenon of seasonal hands cultivating reflection –
visitation of these in accompaniment with time, past,
particularly energies and imagination, spent –
fences are already down, dawn awaking –
stepping through.

September 24, 2013
thoughts on rising, early, five-six am
in my rooms, darkness outside, giving over to glorious light –

old, Southern airs, these, together with familiar childhood hymns,
    not audible, but in silent repertoire –

    unillicited, natural smiles, the face not
    prostituted, but my pleasure–
        warm gratitude –

   the quelling of selected struggle, quaint placement
    in "the great chain of being" –

Petition

I am alone, I am dry, I am empty;
Holy Presence –
in the earth, the sky, the mountains
and in low valleys;
yet, in the coming water,
and the resting rock – Thou –
be with Thy humble creation,
Thy diligent husbandwoman –
Thy Soul of Thy Soul;
and, bring peace out of pain,
give strength from weakness,
let all joy follow greatest sorrow.

August 4, 2013
in deepest night,
near four o'clock am

– awake, great pain and angst –

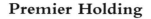

Premier Holding

The day had achieved its fullest hour,
past midday, and the glass burst forth
too bountiful to receive,
for all outdoors in golden splendor
found entrance to my rooms.
My inertia shattered, my awareness
tasting a coquettish grape,
I wished to run into the sunlight – to dance,
in its glory abundance, to bathe, touch and strew,
to enjoy completely in imbibing this holy manifestation of good.
Shadows, as small, tenuous secrets,
softened the composition, creating an ambiance of content
with gentle fowl, quieted, those which,
just, earlier, had heralded the growing bright –
these, in absolute awe, silent of that
of their audible announcing:
– a moment of complete beauty, to hidden, imaged thought.
I will, then, in all joyfulness,
take its gold and twine it about my temples –
to stand, more a "lesser god,"
into a lost full of days.

April 26, 2013
transcribed about eight o'clock pm
after walking into sunlight in early afternoon,
in my breakfast room –

Elizabeth Analysis\Afterthought

-further, I can walk barefoot in warmth
through my fiefdom inside this golden painting,
among hanging berries, promising,
and blossoms outings birthing buds;
and in the walk, I can gather memory of purist beauty and weep
that my humble path has stepped into a complacency
a coined mundanity, poor inside a wealthy season,
a premier holding,
out ancient prescription.

Revisited May 6, 2013
Discretion "...the Better Part..."

Growing, now advancing – very personally contained –
bears a penchant to wander into reverie,
quite apart from the polite, the decorum, the "better part."
The need is almost always declared quickly,
recognizing and approaching a "better" stance
in present arrangements.
In place finds beauty, lost, in decorum, "better,"
reaching, touching; appointing, arranging, knowing –
inappropriately. These company, their mundanely difficult,
unmoving, the smallest monument –
the fullest decorum –
What then of valor:
Achille's grief of his beloved Pathoklos,
dead in Troy's ruin, chose death with honor and glory –
the decision of life in youth
which pens the past, with its instruction –
toward decision: persuasion unto life –
immortal plume and papier! Call out to me that record
be made of the wealth in the past,
beauty and gentle truth, repeatedly,
usurping the "better," the choice of we "lesser gods."

decorum given over to fullest valor,
it in carriage that of olden good
and reason's beauty –

June 6, 2013
in deepest night

a difficult verse to "pen out," although I was certain of my theme;
we live timorously, with every insurance:
but what have we lived. I do wish I were not so much a risk-taker,
or overmuch rebellious toward the conventional,
the concrete mundane – if silently or passively aggressive so –
a deep conflict, at times, near to a grave cleavage –
yet, loss of all comforts to our species, or nearly
so, at times – and irredeemable –

Absolute Glory

From the balcony of my bedroom, I bent to
the morning's gifts, all safe inside
the absolute glory of autumn's smile;
bright yellow, but gentle in its movement,
his grapevine spoke his face, his words –
and I wept at the humble legacy of these
twenty-one years.
The splendored past, rising out summer-warm
Gardenia, a full thousand of them, tortured
my spirit, but, in truth, gave to me the
strength to, again, mourn, the sweetness to
remember – and oh, Richard, the
distance where you now bide is closeted inside
my heart, awake, a season of beauty
from lonely painting, a season of instruction
from the only knowing.

The reality of now, in these such moments,
come up like angel proclamations –
and if not, I do not want to know –

Elizabeth
November 17, 2013
early Sunday morning

– from my bedroom in "Elizabeth's golden fiefdom" –
the autumn morning is in full queenly dress, and with temperate
climes about – all is fragranced by memory's
Sweet Olive, in citrine shadows,
purposing a very moment –

In such related moments, better, easier to hold
to the beauty of past relationships,
especially when beauty can be remembered inside impossible
circumstances. And although we appear
more fanciful than reasonable,
"In matters of the heart, reason does not comply." Such is the
strength of us mortals, we "lesser gods."
— perhaps the wiser weltanschauung to embrace —

The Greatest Alone

I am in the greatest alone, again, in the
winter of January,
when hearts bind together as with
feather and wool;
but I have no covering, only my thought
alone, and my thought — a red Poppy of old
Provence — a sunset hued Camellia
from a once-loved hand — perhaps there rolls out
the shooter marble, to cries of excited
pleasantry —
Can the heart find peace in thought, or
recollection of steps out almost
purist sentiment —
I think the raindrops without winter stars
are closing the watch of my heart's
most need, and ought left to sleep remaining night
to the draught of immeasurable fatigue.

Elizabeth
in deepest night
near two o'clock, am, January 17, 2013

An Impromptu of Nothing

The coming in of the day's closing hours;
projects laid to their keeping;
and medicinal routines in proper order —
ought now but to wait the
coming in with the window
that frees of pain, lays aside care, and,
perhaps, will offer a dalliance with dreams,
or some humble pleasantry.
Small grows the radiance of the lights to the feast;
however, it is, yet, chosen, and will remain,
placed with the joys of
heaven.

Sad, though, and difficult, that the dolls must, and cannot
but shadow, a full cognizance of the struggle,
even into a portion offering a peace dressed in the
rags of acceptance.

I remember the long, incredibly difficult days of summer school
in my junior and senior years of college — how dull, how
plodding — these — how without any apparent imagina*tion* — *life
in some of the readings, those depicting the school of
realism in American Literature — Zona Gale, in her Miss Lula Bett,*
with continued reading, draws an impossible view of a limited,
stifling life, largely unknown to the participants: mundane,
slow, and without fire or passion —
insidiously alone — so the narrative
appeared.

The color was gray, the soundings of summer locusts,
continuous, in schedules, repetitive;
I tried, desperately, to transpose some of my sentiments into the
piece, to give it a semblance of life as I knew and dreamed it
to be – joy, movement, beauty, dashes of the absurd – fire of my
then latent illness – to "burn, burn" in the business of living.
Now, in these quiet, necessary moments, I can realize the keen
insights Ms Gale observed of life in the
Midwest, yet in the deep south.
Will and circumstance spar continuously,
and will is not always the victor,
or, if, in this exhibition of behavior, the players
emerge victorious, they are, yet,
lost.

It is one of the great sadnesses of life that we are capable of looking
beyond, into pastures and meadows, into thought and principle,
into sentiment and resolve, only to bow, ultimately, to the force of
natural law.

Elizabeth
-- thoughts, in deepest night –
October 17, 2013

The reference to the phrase "It is one of the great
saddnesses of life …," is from the French writer,
Chateaubriand, in his work, Attala –
champion of the innocence of the new world, and the
"noble savage" –

Fairest Hours

The fairest hours are coming forth,
those of conclusion, and of new beginnings;
of confession, and its redemption.
Within these moments the questions and journeys compressed
into their grande arms — inside which we find
knowings and acceptance —
out the assessing which gather the ponderings,
the thoughts — these pass to the side, within, into yesterday,
the glory of its holdings, the strength and power it affords.
And where do answers, the true conclusions,
which make possible —
in grande certainty — new beginnings, lie
— in the all of it, for our lives are,
in their portions, together, complete, and our selves
speak the wisdoms we seek.
It is with good reason, balanced sentiment, and
thoughtful prayer — a holy communion — that we
"look before and after," but, truly, not to
pine, but to purpose, with gratitude, to embrace
the moment, its beauty and absolute power, to
gather the fields of glory, the longings of our spirit,
whether stepping forward into tomorrow — or into the
hindward, into yesterday — all — it arranging into the good,
complete in the moment, our passionate now,
our eternity, to be in ever thanksgiving.

Elizabeth
into new day
December 20, 2013
storms, about —

— gurus, consultants, formulae, folk wisdom, and research —
these help, but do not best the challenge ever occurring of looking
forward to fulfillment, and into the past to find
noble instruction in peace —

thoughts, in these final days of a requiring,
but giving year —

Early Morning Fragment

Awareness came into, and among, fresh
expectancies,
breaths in the moment
entering me into the joyful feast.

Saying farewell to night included gratitude,
its fingers, in softest manipulation,
having played out the days of my
heart,
being lost to some, and worthy in yesterday,
gathering altogether truth or
surmise —
to be turned about, soonly, by dreams from my
Mountain.
The day was kept aside, heavily, as a bride
in her chamber, but the excitement was burdensome,
left to hours appearing of courage and
jousting with the unconsciously heavy, strong,
and difficult — one with the
unfortunate ….

a dream–like recounting while coming out of small, deep morning
sleep, somehow knowing thoughts of worth,
trying to record, but not being able, could not — at least correctly —
I have words and have, here, captured what may have been
in my thought, probably, to be set, still, to the aside —
such moments allow me to review thoughts at different levels —
these not being fully accessible to conscious thought —

Elizabeth
May 22, 2013
early morning, about six-thirty am

Cleopatra's Musings
on
Antony's Horse

Let me feel the heaviness of a crimson coverlet,
sewed of crushed velvet, underbound
of golden satin – this soft – this softest heaviness
of love, your touch of tender care.

In the lullaby of thy round-toned voice,
surely waters falling from highest mountains,
let the natural berceuse whisper to my
gentle, wanting self, finding safety and peace.

Yet, let tears press their way, as summer pears,
sunset-hued, constricted of fullness with the wealth of
confections' sweetness, to fragrance smiling beautylove,
the breath of love and of the beautiful.

And when I am content in genuine loveliness, in legendary
amour and the full drape of springtime's
cherry-snow – come to me, and wound me with
thy tendernesses, that I become as soft mist, to
rest upon thy petaled eyes, so that they know the pleasant,
weightless dark of peaceful sleep.

– And if these measures of passion and care should falter in their
offerings toward the pleasing they wish to bring –
let their, then, sorrow weep, together,
that of the the abounding world
of night, ever, that their true sentiments find,
in these weepings, only, an acceptable comfort in
their release.

Elizabeth
midnight, passed
October 29-30, 2013
an aware, needing fancy –

In this, my composition, some vocabulary,
images, and philosophical constructs
could be attributed to J. Donne, and his
great, unfulfilled, personal needs;
his techniques are also of interest, one being
juxtaposition, using spiritual
(Christian) against physical (carnal).

A Fancy, On Love

I do not know my love, he has no name,
yet, more, there s not any presence — any thread of identification.
I know — from my darkened grotto, of all my secrets —
that inside my knowing is the stalwart self
I grieve to hold,
the bolden heart, while full with care.
Between, we would share gold, but not a care,
a dependence, and the upward "orifice," honored;
we would find the bindings of joy in
interest and skills — the harp,
the blade, the falcon;
books of wisdom, and travel in lands which
offer languages, beautifully sounded,
and the full history if our kind.
Beside would find the study of the beauty of
particular evidences of man's glory,
the tendernesses of mothers, and the difficult
ability to crush the infant kitten,
attending its dam,
in circumstances, calling.
Most, perhaps, would be the property of reciprocity,
allowing all selves to follow their true
way — in this virtue would lie the key to the gem- studied belt,
and passion would pour out its flame of fullest fire.
Ah, my pen has said my heart, and I press the words —
surely akin to Petrarch's sonnets — to my breasts —
to hope, and to trust the finding of all beauty,
and true content.

Elizabeth
drawn in deepest night, May 19, 2013
intense rain showers, the pretending,
shy growling of the friendly cur –

I know the description is, in part, adolescent, a fancy, improbable,
but the saying of my heart's innocence, if worn by
adventures in its ever seeking.

May 10, 2013, in deepest night
intense rain showers, the pretending, shy
growling of the friendly cur

An Ambiance

Just before the afternoon's two o'clock,
the dying summer sun smiled
with a kind of silence
on the old, now partially retired funeral home,
it resting quietly in my gaze, as I
entered the small southern hamlet;
the smile brought gathering images, many and
more, spliced between thoughts of sombre
nature, however alongside the
relieved sigh that no one was dead,
at least no one in the patronage of the
aging establishment.
We "can't go home again," but we do, after a
fashion, all in our own way, if only within
an ambiance;
and such circumstance was good – that no one
had died, but sadness found, for many
already had died, and now have been assigned
to images, distant, and prescribed a sentiment –
oh, please – let the real, the true – the "objective
aware," let these escape my thought's capture,
lest they perish me with their
whole strength.

Elizabeth
September 11, 2013
thoughts on entering Brookhaven for a hair-cut,
turning left at the first stop sign (the old funeral home),
past leaving the interstate –

Darkened More

Do woods decay, do vapors weep, or can it be that
all, together, we are weary, and cannot see a
new beginning, a casting off, to experience in ornamental flair,
a pleasantrie, in
beautiful robes, in new and beautiful climes.
The casting off is difficult
for our own becoming, that in the physical,
because it indexes the power of earthy life; but, perhaps,
the verity marks smaller, or, in some sense,
larger, in that our spirits know, more, that the advent of
conclusion is early, and long, in its processing,
reminders pulling away joy with every
exchange.
With every arc and path beyond, we are,
if reflective,
cognizant of the possibility
of rarer splendor, purer glory, at the
conclusion of the casting off – youth's strength,
his will and dreams – all playing out of the
perishing of the physical – for the spirit has other
worlds to wander about, not being
dependent on fleshly power for direction, or
traversement.
And then, the twine begins its final circumference –
the becoming, truly, only in spirit, being
without pattern or known form, other than in surreal
images conjured up out dark and great, primordial
silence, in which the first, and concluding
universes visit, and sometimes merge.

We, then, approach the decay without help,
the weeping without solace, altogether in the
frightening reality of the totally
unfamiliar.
In the become, then, existential,
how do we pleasure, after any variety, that of which we have no
knowledge, no intuition, no direction without
sponsoring:
we stand naked before the entire
unfamiliar, without anchor, within true darkness which,
if lighted, could offer no past from which to draw, and
therefore no present, feigning a future, in this lack.

New robes, then, are doned, without joy, or the
tease of a Francesca bliss —
without, more, any
consolation, hope, or peace
in pitching one's tent.
And there is no wisdom which assures new robes, or
becoming into contentment, other those of
terrestrial seasons, but only the truest knowing
of a vast, dark plain on which we are bent in blind despair,
made intolerable by selected remembrances,
coming finally to experience the concluding
ingredient in loss — that of acceptance.

Elizabeth
in deepest night
September 15, 2013
thoughts out great fatigue, pushing me toward more
dark, than I often feel —

Down turning Thought

How pleasing the shores of Avelyon,
sweet maids bringing into;
sisters mist and ash, your quietly taking away —
how very so —
and I, the limberlost moth,
beautiful, yet, but wounded, more —
how radiant, how true the leaping of your
flame —
near to, near to, not an aside —
near to, near to, the petaled reality of, now,
a seemingly dark;
true, so — true, so — the glory in the light
to the she-wolf of the magnificent hind leg,
but is she not more legend than true —

Elizabeth
down turning of thought, tonight, from where I truly bide,
and in the biding, alone,
save of wine from faintest love —
in shadows —
past the season of alone.
March 8, 2013
near eight o'clock pm

in this moment, this moment accusing eternity,
I am alone, alone of myself, most,
taking cues to being from stimuli that
falls into my unfortunate space;
how to get back to anywhere — any something;
without some success, all has found, has made its own alone —

Do I write from being alone, or the stage (condition) in
habituation —

Embroidered Moment

— roses into remembrance ;
— as shadow quietens the glorious round of bright;
— the bounty of camaraderie comes to rest,
in prescribed review,
and the "length of days" falls to shouting the distance,
resting, already in place -
Consciousness, in clever maneuver, finds the constructs
"maturity," and "adjustment," quite open to discussion;
and the overpowering, the absolutely magnanimous
gift of knowing, within being, is politely relegated to the
academic - fire and passion, honor and fealty - becoming
empty in polite conversation, to be forgotten when slipping
into routine and familiar patternings.
October, brilliantly blue and wide, in good rapport with
the latent excitement of coming festivals -
Ah, the child in the tapestry of self, fold over the adult, and
give to us all, the splendor of the regal, anciently
embroidered moments in their nativity.
Elizabeth, in deepest night – - October 18-19,2013

Elizabeth in deepest night
October 18-19, 2013

Crossing Over

And with the falling of the medicinal drop, and with the
taking of knowing thought – each occurring near objective
climes, my maidenhood was, then, reborn, refashioned,
after a flower, lady to the very sun, lord to whom I am now meted;
how like a veil pulled from my forehead, that so to
reason, accompaniment to given
love.
I was, altogether, the maid of the slipper of glass, and sooted rags
turned to garments of purist gold threads.
And these with stones, not of telling color,
form, comely, or fragrance
sweet, but my new estate beared forth its
wealth in company, dear, of those both grande, and good,
the absolute replica of humanity walking
past its coins, and stones, past courage and rolling fields,
the vineyard readying its glory; but in path
to humanity that needed, and was, instead, visited and
given, having been crossed over, towardwards, by
one of its own, to the other side.

Elizabeth
October 26, 2013
four fifty-eight am

Waking suddenly, in the first hours of morning, my left eye,
of infection's clasp, and the heavy monotony of sleep — such
left me in pain and impotence to open to new day.
Seeing, first, in construct, and then, in execution, a hand
appeared to my inner knowing, to place a
balm, an oil or, perhaps, an herb, into the fated
eye; and I, again, at once, saw and
felt redemption's sweetness, as the first,
again, and the fancied Samaritan
voicing the heard of the birthright of us
all, in full humanity's guise.

Out reverie of soul —
butterflies, a menagerie of colorful bright, of
joy, from ancient, Eastern lore, flew
as cascading roses, down a wall — joy, over and over, all.

In recording this waking experience, I feel to have
bound together the light of two or, more,
three cultures into the whole we ever were, are.

"...Were Paradise ....."

The passing moments of absent love
share the lovely chambre of
waiting seasons;
always to express, to find, to be in their
banishment from the aware, to bear in their distance
the living, in truth, waiting their fullest being –
It is with longing of the streams, the portals,
those of memory, that the full of a sentiment becomes, truly,
ours; the truth etched into the urn is masterful,
and its source cannot be bested,
but would, can – consciousness, in maneuver select and rare,
offers Rachel in the person of Leah.
Dressed in reality, revisited; fragranced by longing; and
gentled with time passed, that which we
hold – not of warm flesh in hand – but in generously, thoughtfully
embellished abiding, in the
giving of full acceptance, the moments
pass to us in the distance of the absent, into the
transmuted ecstasy of the present, more,
the recorded past, with all
"bountiful" condiments of reflection.

The fading echo, the descending, paling sigh –
with the imagined – ah, "..... were paradise ......"

Elizabeth
thoughtful in moments before sleep – alone – but
beautifully in company –
October 23, 2013
in deepest night –

In It All

In it all, is, full mystery,
the searching glance of the hound which
hears mixed commands;
and, in it all, is, full clarity –
the favored playfellow that has all gestures offered,
relevant, calling out biding trust.
Yet, in it all, is struggle – thoughts,
behaviors, allegiances and haunting fears,
and, still, dreams –
such is crowding in, in silent movements,
quiet which extends, in beauty that, in its fullest
largess, evokes sentiment –
or more, in its passing:
the familiar is sweet, if but security for that
novel, for we think, to assume prediction,
follows, therefore, control.
The unfamiliar threatens in the resulting
lack of comfortable prediction, projection, prognosis –
Andso – of life – most of struggle – for seers,
gurus, of whatever varieties; insurance, investments,
of whatever credentials; budgets and schedules, of
personal choice – these leave, still, in
lying down and rising up, within robes of hope
and doubt – midst "Happy birthday;" "Happy anniversary," –
and "...many more!"
– a finding of mystery, "left wanting," in that of it all.
We cannot know, and so we do not know:
to plan, to venture, to find peace in full knowing,
of anything.

Only the boon of faith, made possible by the
maneuver of denial, can the struggle be quieted –
ought left is unthinking, slothful dalliance – ultimately the
waste and despair of cowardly, unexamined acceptance –
for we are all Dantes who can, on occasion,
stand out, to intuit, to know, under distant,
heavenly stars.

Elizabeth
November 15, 2013
two forty-five am

– long, long thoughts following my final chore

before bedtime – finishing my complete review of
all verses written, that are extant – these for publication ;
none are published, presently, other than some
several caught up in earlier works.
There are many variations,
the muse being quiet creative, in loveliness
and composition.
They, each, or most often, are centered on this theme, just
behind (whatever its finished hue),
as has been such the total of the years of
my life, since the emerging
of formal operational thought (abstract thinking), and
believed shadowing before, when my moods
were given over to lack of understanding.

Elizabeth

The "stars of Dante," above, is a "phrase" which refers to all men,
from his grande Medieval work, "The Divine
Comedy," part "The Inferno,"
representing God's presence and love –

Effervescent Day

The quiet that I hear becomes an acceptable
fellowship of familiar, ringing bells,
thousands of them, sand grains in
movement; as my geese, from the south
woods, early, these were quite unpleasant, but now arrive,
attractive guests, generous to my
attention.
– For my thought entertains cruel existentials,
those which challenge my will with
their particulars;
and my silver taunts my memory of raven
so that I drift into speculation:
before senium, time holds as a glorious quest,
given audience, fully rich and
satisfying; the years, once achieved, however,
bear most the continued, splendid struggle,
but with great reflection –
establishing, then, recognition, with hope
brought forward, yet, a resting, gathering
forth an anticipation for the day, its cloth spread
out before,
filled with joy of the radiant peacock,
the constant rainbow –
the ever, virgin dewfall.

The fragrance of the fading rose, positioned
above the poor piano we children knew,
references an imaged road, too long, a path
attending full intensity, and its cohorts, they to
grow into the complete.
How unfortunate, how filled with grief,
the joy to life – how sadly we experience the
truly beautiful only through questions
and rejection of the feast: that inside hours passed
into the effervescent day.

Pressing our realities for a small portion of generous,
left-over beauty is greatly difficult;
perhaps the passing of time and the
rearranging of the characters who, together, play out the

intimate road to which we are all heirs –
– could, such will offer thoughtful self-perusal,
become the only conclusion left to us
"lesser gods."

– questioning of the proverbial journey,
itself, its beauty and pathos, absolutely deluging all thought,
usurping the joy of the feast – We, then, – attempt –
through loveliness – through the acceptance of
all, even the lonely, grey-blue heath,
the giving Quasimodo's,
the death of the once radiant rose –

Elizabeth
March 15, 2013

the piece arrives, having been worked
though a number of days filled with
questionings inside the beauty of another, come,
spring: how much the need for a "safe place," without
the necessity of acceptance and the "road's" multitudinous
requirings.

– truly a "romantic" sentiment, "my "entering fragrance" –
but my thoughts this day –

I find that confections do not always adequately repair the
press of necessary evil.
note, after transcription of verse
today, March 16, 2013
eventide

the "bells" hallucination is now an old, familiar one, and not
angst producing; it does portend the slightly "askew"
pattern of the piece, much of it written in the deep of night,
early morning of March 15-16, and worked through in the
evening of March 16, – with difficulty understanding my
thought of the night before.

A Fair Histoire

In afternoon hours of pretending, autumn
sighings,
I am fallen, close in bed, to run
the distance of
purging awareness;
come this given – of he or she who lies closest on my breast,
I find with these, in often, covered moments,
greatest distances, in worded
pictures which wander through my
thought, with windows, not of tears, but
wet of true sorrow.
Does the awareness fountain from my knowing,
lack of fullness; do those who are
in these separate, many vignettes of ivory,
pure, or perhaps, with stains of crimson –
do these know more than I – in my own miserable,
wretched, only vignette –
Will reassessing in the fallen drape of the
quieted night, when fears congregate
beside dreams –
will this time restore, or further murder the
innocent.
If, thereby, in the spilling of blood – and always
there be some, fallen, in togetherness – close to come –
if such will be, to, then, vanquish –
no matter the dishonor –
– loss dresses every warrior,
and left to the aside are those who view, and,
with conscious good will, reconstruct – a fair
histoire.

Elizabeth
August 3, 2013
following a day of inconsistencies, irony, misunderstandings
and greatest dissonance; questionings of my own
spirit and relationships with others
require great effort at wholeness —

First Goldenrod, 2013

Today, goldenrod, its very roadside sea,
laughed yellow bright
into the high, and azsured sky.
And in my heart I felt the press of
passing time, back through the short
distance to its sweetest memory.
Hours have been given over to the good,
annivesaried by these tender images:
encouraging of friendship, and the devotion
toward kin; signaturing documents, with
arrangements to be put in place;
effort in finding faith, a strong and
purposed bark —
and listening to the varied voices, the sighs
of my giving heart.
The skiff of self finds deep its road, and turbulent
its flowing path, as days move toward
conclusion;
eyes and fingers, together, with idea, will one day
move their touch in the all unfamiliar,
and goldenrod will, its reality, and memory,
be dark in its tomorrow —
laughing, yellow bright to become a fable, a legend
to those, only, whose steps remind forebearers
having passed over, already, their familiar path,
these "golden, earthly sands."

Elizabeth
eventide
August 25, 2013

in a quiet moment, remembering a field of early, beautiful
goldenrod en route home from the grocer (Kroger) —
goldenrod, since childhood, in autumn — a gift from my parents —

I Will Hold

I will hold my hand,
one with the other,
to open and close my arms about
my self, alone –
then to weep upon my arm,
that night has come,
and
none will warm me throughout
its long adventure.
None will enter, no one to reach
his touch and encircle the
great of my wintry cleanness,
or take my hand – to be his
"gentle playfellow," as fabled
Cleopatra to her Anthony –
then, to enter the hidden path
of darkened wealth,
the crowning, biding tryst with
covered thought.

Elizabeth
July 3, 2013
near bedtime –

With Unclear Notes

And in my rooms, I find the accusing knowing
that I am pilgrim to their very familiarity;
always to ponder, I struggle with the absolute
marvel of seeing, it so much the prostituting
urchin to my orthodox self.
I read for clarity, but my senses divide so that
I look forward to first error, to misunderstanding-
becoming cognizant that I hope,
fervently, these, not to be; with innocent,
prophetic will, I too, listen, only to finish
spoken statements, to certain that the proper is
correctly said, that projection of my own flaws
and lesser abilities find quiet, and understanding.
Pitiable, most, to myself, fall long glances
on the beautiful – but not to rest, for great angst
in finding a corruption in its fair.
Who am I, where, yet should I be, journey toward –
I am neither physician nor cleric,
not husbandman to any humble fiefdom;
my wisdom is uncelebrated, my strength,
if given attention, even less.
The cloth is, then, laid aside to bare the source
of my all wanderlust, for it is of this matter,
in its complete – all – that my journey is continuous.
The heart hunts a peace, wholeness in which
care is spreaded out, and contentment, Everyman's portion.
Ah, HolyFatherGod, flow out my pen words
that heal, and let me hear, fully, the worst,
camaraderie with Lear's plaintive sigh –
that my heart find solace in the wholeness of the broken,
the unfinished, the inept attempt –
the false assessment; may the untrained voice find,
in its unflowered searchings, the glory in Thy will to me.

June, 2013
after several weeks of thoughtful writing (unclear notes)
alone with thoughts of our true "condition,"
the unhappy steps we struggle with in its difficulty –
written in statements, broken by sleep,
after grave "ponderings" following a very productive,
if "stretching" visit with John –

Streaming

Being lovely is truly lovely, as a golden touch
or engraved coin holding wealth within their own.
Suffering hewns into beauty extraordinaire – andso what of stripes,
insults, rejection; unkindnesses – of all wounds -
these being, becoming true good inside the seams of
continuous circumstance.
Prunings and waiting in absence are included in
the drawing: the pastoral, the select and rare,
the gentle scene of sighs and passionate visions of love,
and warmth – zephyrs in the afternoons -
luted songs among thoughts of deepest sentiment -
to come, quickly, weeping and loneliness,
downcast struggles and the drawing of shape
from man, and flesh.
Coming, then, is speculation of the very good -
it becomes a tenderness in bruising, a joy out knowing,
love revisited in absence -
a sure cultivation in night.
If this be the way of understanding, joyful glancing
toward the come blush, into radiance,
of the pomegranate's brought loveliness,
its form would come to shame in theory of the processing,
aging lesser.
To know the lost glory in autumn, under the scepter of time,
to become the sprout, the leaves -
spring bringing, another -
the hunger in life then poses as a formidable postulate.
To hold most is great the loss, and happiness
in all lifts away with our sun.
What we find, we have taken, and that of knowing,
hangs the knot of unhappy evaluation;
out all the moments emerges the gallant knight
of acceptance, having been in all principled company –

May–June 2013
written in and out of sleep, a salad of thoughts
and poor scripting of text –
could some – much maganification – many
images, lost and recovered –

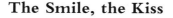

The Smile, the Kiss

The principle in place, in cognition's realm,
that such as mystic, lunar in widest seas,
knows then to our spirits the sometimes smile,
brevity's child, opening between fair roses hue,
it of scarlet's wealth, for a season.
We do not smile into eternity, nor kiss away
the formidable dragons of time and natural law,
but find content in the living present,
the altered moment, all of ever captured,
if we are freed by the sweet bondage of knowing.
Ah, the hand that reaches across in these select exchanges,
grasps a portion of the immortal,
the players attired in raiment of angels;
and taken away from thee at potent centras
of wielding eternis, makes grande, again,
even more, the smiles of we "lesser gods."

September 8, 2013
in deepest night
− just a thought, on slipping away into
sleep, following a quite special
celebration of my birthday –

Suddenly...

Suddenly, in a rare moment, the "toys"
in my bedroom came away from their backgrounds,
and, in the lamp light, gave me
blessing for the night.
Their beauty, and truth, became acknowledgment of my spirit,
my hands and thought, in movement and color;
the joy of the feast embraced me,
and all else before became as parenthetical,
an appositive which did not challenge or shadow.

January 4, 2013
just at bedtime, about eleven thirty-five pm

afterthought

O Winter, give back to me the industry
of self so that all that has been,
and is to come, be, part of mine –
yesterday, tomorrow – merely constructs to help
embellish present hours, with wisdom and beauty.

Today, in my bedroom, among the shadows
of wintry afternoon, I saw a masculine image, grande,
and metaphorical – I am not as well,
presently, as in most days, a problem I must
address with John, on Monday, next.

The Vera Question

We stand inside the shadow of death,
all our moments, as we are, ever,
in the glow of effervescent life;
and in the moments between, yet, into,
lies a dissonance, the scourge of all our days.
The departing that taunts the sparkling wine,
golden mead before the piercing –
such recounted, remembered and the blush of fragrant,
dusty rose, above its gentle histoire,
to speak throughout its day of brilliant sun–
Does salvation forgive the sting? – ah yes –
but the journey into salvation – surely the dragon
of its requiring manifests mortal,
to our gifted spirits, aware.

February 5, 2013
mid-morning, following a night and early morning
of great angst and soulful questioning –

When Hearts Speak...

I have buckled my shoes,
I have collected my coins, and I stand with angst and joy
to the reaching of the feast.
Long, long the eternity of the moment –
painted clay, and beloved holdings of infinite variety –
that which hands can do at the heart's request –
these visit, embrace, in constant giving –
no death to, in time, cloud into dark;
but hearts who speak to the presence of we
"lesser gods," these allow us to harbor, truly,
to find a measured content.

February 9-10, 2013
in deepest night – about one-thirty am
some content not quite clear – but - "as it came" –

Our Nights

With a fresh blink of marble blue, day came in –
out the smooth, endless void of dark,
a holding of consciousness,
both strange and beautiful.
Together, like spectre partners, truth and half–truth,
had moved through a verilea, macabre,
leaving unrest, and sentiments in dissonance.
Dark flowers had hung about so that light became,
quickly, antagonistic to what was a long, long quieting, journeying
in thought, inside small, filled apartments which kept secrets
telling most of who we are.
Our secrets require fancy, surreal exaggerations,
and unthinkable images, these flying away,
together, with unrecognizable leanings,
except somewhere in a consciousness which
haunts us in waking hours.
There is no fold in the drape of night which
is comfortable other that which dulls
the knowing while unknowing.
Ought but to stand amazed in our own presence,
the select beings we are, empowered by will
and wonderfully structured mass,
to joust with our own, most, intimate knowings –
when the sun, in its western dim,
allows more cognizance of self
than the opium dens of old England towne.
Caught – how fearful, yet tender our nights –
with dreams and wisdoms from our Mountain;
feasts, and pleasure – alongside the extended, angstful
thoughts into yesterday, and more, tomorrow –

May 18, 2013
following a night whose repertoire of dream included those
harsh and cruel, tender and sweet –

Night Confessional

I am finishing, and I am sorrowful,
for so appears that all properties show erosion,
save, perhaps, individual wisdom.
Sounds enter all about, surreal, but, then,
who can ever know the art, now, of listening.
My joy is in waking, but the hours arrive
to conclusion in each frame.
Mirrors press, calendars chide, yet the feast days
of all peoples speak to me, as well.
Come, come, peace, solitude when individual
perceptions are as correct as those
of the celebrated mystic.
We are our own prophets, and I cannot but say:
I will lie among firm stones, and these
punctuated by thorns and writhing,
speckled eels – my choice which was not ever chosen -
I will dance my own, as Isodora,
and into the night; I will think until
I feel more strangely than before;
mushrooms might satisfy, but candles
can add the bowing call -
It may be that vanity is salvation to us,
if it can bear its foundation in the distance.

October 9, 2013
in deepest night
before, and after an episode of Rheumatoid
inflammation, pounded by cares of other complextion -

Today, Complete

A completed day – today: waking into full cognizance -
everything in sameness, but, truly, all, different -
this knowing called out, again, my separateness -
that this grey knowing found, lost, the camaraderie
with the great f others, and – that they dragged along
their own, individual sacks of stones:
in this moment – such touched me, very little;
my brief, but grande confession wounded me,
and, still, its truth stood, reality.
I felt myself to know the massive,
compounded folly we attempt -
I thought of my perceptive malaise, with me these years,
and I wished to cry out -
I must to weep – the bitter – to say my pain of
thought and sentiment – and Thee, John,
came to me in an offering, just of late;
somehow, I touched my stones and that of Thee was enough -
that I had ought – just words – for a genuine troth -
I rose to the day that has been, and it has,
in its true, been good.

January 27, 2013
difficult day, but His directive -
pain transmuting into beauty -

Oh, Joy – Nien

More and more, yet, less the days,
hours giving the beautiful of its holdings to me:
still, all concludes, less the heavy breath of knowing -
yet, in the sunlight, all remains, true, beautiful, and long.
Perhaps it is this thought which strikes the failing
blow to full constancy, it, beside living flesh within
the path of time, an arranging which allows a Morpheus
respite to those who grow less in their awareness.
Andso such, the paling light,
as is the shroud of awareness, fallen about our moments,
becomes, to, if it would sound, lift into the company
of all souls, and we would drift, islands of self,
caught of a bark, to know, again, the certain glory
of our day, such a very hermitage, the established environment
in place – these left to embrace a fated reservoir,
announcing – couldso – a plenty – to be part of the wager.
Light, of light: come early, in friendly spaces,
together with the portioned moment; come into, more,
as a lover, to enjoy, afar, and also in the moment,
but all between rests the lover's fantasy; to be concrete,
would be to lift the (mortal) to moments of finding.
Oh, joy – nien – the blade strikes true:
time gives that that it requires -
this – the shadow of us "lesser gods" -

December 7-8, 2013
in deepest night, so that I do not concept most of the piece -
I think that I was under the influence of
musings regarding the power of the
moment in experience, whenever or with
whatever – but to know the futility
of all, yet the beautiful, as much strength as it possesses.

Today's Pippa

The sun shone joyful, early today,
and lighted music fell about;
I became his natural Pippa, and the world was,
in every turn, toward the right.
September songs are bittersweet by –
as a delicious confection –
being away, almost immediately –
present, tasting – but within its passing.
In my Pippa guise, then, to, of certainty,
be left wanting – of the moment's beauty -
and surely, yet – though as dew fall in its
effervescence, I am content to be within,
to hold, and then to wait, in grateful remembrance.

September 11, 2013
mid-morning, a beautiful September morning -
pause to – in awe and wonder, be thankful -

"hindward glances"

From *Beauty and Spirit*

Thou art my nourishment, the lamp unto my feet;
poor wretch that I am, I continue to need
Thy manifested Presence.
My petition, at this moment, is for more
recognizable Presence, which, in Its Being,
shows the child, yet infant, I am – that I am.
I ask for more inward confidence of my faith,
that it be seen in my activities, and without angst or foreboding.
Give to me images, as humble as they may be,
some, likely, not to ever know scripting again.
Of Thy Presence I, perhaps, might be thought to be unsure,
(as when I speak of hearing the bells),
but Thou will be, at least, reasonable –
full of love and understanding.
Give me, Holy Presence, the ability to access my faith,
and live in all goodness and happiness,
a true bird in flight –
free in the bondage of Thy gentle Presence.

Early Spring, 2013
in deepest night
these lines were written late in the night,
under heavy pain medication;
much is unclear, and I have improvised, today, in the transcribing –
the notebook was a gift from Tonia
the period in which these lines were written was that of the stress
fracture in my right tibia –

The Conclusion

When lights begin to halo, and, outside,
insects have softened their voice,
the sounds of roads heard,
only intermittently -
I sense, again, the conclusion of the day,
begun long into a distance now -
from a soft fire lighting the inside of morning,
forward to fullness, and the advent of movement,
into the westward dim.
Thoughts drift about, but most often,
they search out the wealth in yesterday, and remembrance;
there is imaging of scales all about — and recordings -
a complete awake of cognizance.
How not to sigh — into the night,
it becoming obedient to fatigue and convention;
perhaps this is the better of our dalliance before we close
the dark, the dying moon against its forgotten heavens.
Every goodbye begins a new adventure, yet,
it is folly t command a principle concluding
balance which has not examined loss -
then, to night — I offer my condolences, for it remains
a wealth, and a beauty, indescribable,
but it stands metaphor to ultimate despair,
save the promise of the slowly progressing brilliance
of heralded day.

August 4, 2013
near midnight, becoming new day -
I, writing of my angst of captured consciousness,
caught by the draught of sleep, bringing the almost
cataleptic state, draped by a waring understanding -
the height of thought — an almost full forgiving,
but awareness, of objective reality -

Prayer

Help in press,
give wisdom in conflict;
I offer praise for good,
adoration of beauty;
give strength with gifts, holding,
balance in difficulties;
and accept all thanksgivings for grace.
Glimpse, me the sunrise, and refresh my temple
with sweet herbs, and rainwater;
call, Thou, my energies, and inspire to bind,
courage with joy.
In all fullness of good content,
of Thy fashioning, breathe on my thy breath of peace,
a sigh at the parting hour.
In loving strength, and in obeisance,
I find grace, security and – healing –
surely the Samaritan revisited.

May 11, 2013
in deepest night
a daily prescription

The Eve

The night around the day bares eve
to saddest thought, for new light brings
its face to the final care of this most recent
ebb and flow of time.
Love has worn its color pale,
but at its seams, shows deepest shade,
entering pathotic contrast, too grievous to carry.
What of days – this bright to dim in shorter steps,
to only carriage through, giving fancies of leather,
soiled of dragons slain, for ladies' smiles -
but to must take off these quieted robes,
to wear the fitting, darkest cloak.
Is found enough in dragons slain,
and ladies' smiles, to exchange for knowing loss -
take sons and daughters into the away;
the kitten dam's dark logic weighs the heavy true.
And the red-gold moon will rise in the very
murder of beautiful form and hue,
to vent its wider killing on thoughts of longer
nights, and hand a fullest drape of grey.
Out windows of flesh and wood, of straw and stone,
the all of death visits tremulous thought;
Ah, Man, Thou "lesser god," know
Thy wisdoms in their grande complete,
that Thy inner eye catch the height of true,
that of the Kitten Dam.

July 31, 2013
after an extended, telling phone visit, in the evening
ten-thirty pm – one o'clock am

Perceptive Climes

Yes — a quickly passing dream,
through haste, and desire,
and angst, as moving shadows –
then, slowly, and quickly, the vocabulary softens,
finding storms, with midnight,
not so much gladiators to be struggled against,
until on blade decides.
And all in the between draws a painting,
a canvas covered of energy spent,
that of movement, lost and saved,
the rainbow coming to be a construct
more pleasing than summer radiance.
Perceptive climes can please, or ill,
yet speak more profitably the realities of our days –
those showing plagues about,
suffering unto dying,
battles out great warrings,
with cries of suffering and victory,
yet marrying and giving in marriage:
ah — that we weave our later garments –
those of thought and flesh –
from that of good, that of sound –
Yes — with the thread of hope into peace –

April 27, 2013
resting at noon

Kept in Place

Metallic gold, and ivory pearl,
these, behind cadmium red light –
with such qualities, I am content in these
"fallen hours," those most froid,
at the early four o'clock –
and these particulars, I know, most, the solitude –
that I am, truly, alone,
to be skewed is novel – at times, a poor circumstance –
but most, a curiosity of needed, distant properties –
if, in truest reckoning, a quaint glory –
and soon, this Thanksgiving Eve,
I will be all that I can be:
too much aware of self,
so that I exist, the purpose of the
ever stalking hound:
victorious, but from all other, lost.

November 27, 2013
four o'clock am
assessing – after rising to paint –

different, not "ungood,"
but, different, good; different – perhaps,
a positive singularity,
to be kept in place –

In All Constancy

The small, yet truly grande,
worlds we wander through,
between dew fall, and dew fall,
filled with our little importances –
these realities bend with heavy grief when they
are placed beside the poignant humanity we carry
within us, without acknowledgment:
a glance which wept its soul within its covering:
the gifted salutary courtesy offered to slothful
appreciativeness; the trust, to most, unaware,
within the innocence of children running,
happily, inside, to ringing school bells –
these garments, Rafael's gleaming white,
we cast aside to the mundane necessity of fueling,
to calculating minutes, calories, with unattractive
parsimony – these grey, interminable.
Glory, oh glory – out our days – could be, could be -
kingdoms with sunlight streaming through friendly windows;
apples falling, gracefully, to their purpose;
and horses' hoofs in gentle cadence on
aged, familiar cobblestones -
come, come, on the morning's dew fall,
linger, yet stay past that of the falling twilight.

October 25, 2013
near midnight
– thoughtful, in fatigue, of "Martha"
duties, preparing for my scheduled
reception celebrating the publication of my eleventh volume,
one of verse, *Seasonal Portions* – this event,
at my home, Elizabeth House,
on Sunday afternoon, October 27-

The description of the simple, desired – yet,
longed for – world of content
through the three descriptive statements
(windows, apples, cobblestones),
is from a favorite passage written by Tolstoy.
"And I Will Live..."

And I will live, in these obscure rooms, nowhere,
in the silence of a thousand ringing bells,
within lighted darkness;
inside the whole freedom of fullest bondage -
for a season – more -
the closing of days.
The feast will commence out glory of past wealth,
at table, alone, yet, of camaraderie, long,
filled of adventure that was – andso, thanksgiving,
and praise of that which has wandered its way;
that which, in absence, fills the grandest of hours.

April 17, 2014
a fragment, in deepest night, on waking, assessing, still -
poor cast-off fish, in early, grey morning,
in New Orleans – in summer,
some summer, past:
the Richard days -

Notes from Deepest Night

My attention was suddenly foraged
for kinder constants;
what has happened to the entire of Jessica's group –
and I noticed an eagerness, while with me,
a whole reveal of thought:
long Sabbath quiet, whole or no –
full, sooted wisdom, the final days of another,
moved aside: shadowed in...
The quiet became a friendly companion;
afterward, I could return my wings for contended pleasure:
you – you – we –
the [emoted geraniums must, more, dim
their passion, more, right back to me:
your son, half the...

July 31, 2013
in deepest night (early morning of passing sleep) –
unconscious bearing truths only
partially understood, in safety –

Three Portions
One

Today has not been a true day:
I have, in reality, been nowhere, I have done nothing,
and I value myself not at all.
The dream of waking to day, of expectancies, and promise –
this dream has died to me, and I am walking back –
to nowhere. When I draw on memory,
I cannot process it; when I look past the hour –
there is an abundance of theory, only,
and when I consider the moment –
it is already empty.
If this "reality" should, somehow,
become a dream to which I awake and consider,
I will be grateful, but irreparably wounded.
The scourge of these moments of nothingness
live on in latent terror of reappearing,
in conjunction with lost strength,
and vision in the present.
How can I write of life –
it has, somehow, in its full,
passed from me.

Weeks of May 16–29, June 20, 2013
not a bound statement, but recorded moments I always find –
yet, sudden, and quickly away – I always "give up" too quickly,
but I am more resolute when I rearrange –

Three Portions
Two

In these early morning hours,
of waking, orienting, choosing -
I find questions, in the entire,
divided into the, certainly, concrete real — or more,
unfortunately, mundane — but requiring;
I have jousted, often, in past times,
with this diversion, and it remains necessary to
the division to which it is separate -
but into which it flows, ever.
I was, then, subject to a morning freedom
of two appetites — one, beauty, and also joy,
almost to escape description — the second,
beyond the requiring of vinegar and thorns -

abstractions into which we can factor requiring acceptance -

early June, 2013
written in one of my "other" levels of consciousness, alert
when partially awake, reality-based thought, tenuous -

Three Portions
Three

Our little importances wander into their
grande forgetfulness,
and our moments arrive in their onliness–
what to do – how to catch into holding,
but to reach, but to clasp,
with the pursuance of Parsifal –
in cognitive acuity, beside romance,
the fancies of the needing self –
flowers, and jewels, victorious smoke
from fabled battles, the relinquishing
freedom of the moving disc:
honor and inside fiefdoms of absolute content –
the rainbow, towardward, the sunset;
twilight, and, then, afterward, the dark.

June 22, 2013
early morning thoughts
first, full day of summer –
gardenias about, yet, the fragrance of a thousand...

Walt and Me

Awareness came into its first of the day,
that of light only now portending –
and the hour was the fabled, morning four o'clock,
that coldest in winter, and in all seasons,
the most still; and, in my ear, alone,
within the ringing of thousands of tiny bells,
furnished the silence, my spoken solitude.
Embracing, covering, balming – my gift of solitude echoed,
the more recent Rogerian principles of my instruction,
he singing the Ancient's profound melodies so that
my self came to the fore, significantly known,
this maneuver now, possible after long,
wrenching hours of thoughtful examination.
And in the moment, the American bard sang no more
than I, the song of myself, this, now,
comfortable, if sometimes troubling experience,
becoming a reaffirmation of the gift of life –
free, independent in thought and sensual expression,
joy in creating, and growing from exchanges with others,
if at times in divergent stances:
at one, truly, to sit at table,
to the very feast of life,
often, and long.
–to this day, to every day – salute!

September 28, 2013
on rising early, to great arthritic pain, after discordant
dreams of my family, but, then, "I start over every day" –

Southern Duels

I cannot know but the lamplight in darkness,
the spontaneous arranging of giving blossoms –
these within the encompassing, together,
of my continuously sounding bells,
inside their silent reality.
These such are unto me all the day, my portion,
all comfort and strength, holding,
and comforting me –
for I am only decorative matter, with them,
in the music of every being.
If joy can be mine, let circumstance be kind,
but in this arrangement, let me know beauty,
alone, in the word, and image, in sound and form;
let fraternity be without effort, yet difficulty, in honor held,
in courage, shown, in passion, felt.
In quiet times, our thought bears free,
and questions found in this milieu of words crowds our
consciousness – be kind, then, lamplight,
the rose, and gardenia – continuous bells –
yet, then – sweet, of flowing, ringing silence –
that these let us come round to capture all in our nets,
that we find, with our seeing,
to know joy of all else, all other,
in the whole strength of our self, alone,
acknowledged.
Let white linen ensembles, in early Southern
dawn, with instruments brought, and dressed,
from afar – let these decide, of question, if such
a construct be made.

May 1, 2013
in deepest night
thinking of the difficulty in long term relationships,
the reality of true self, alone –
"All Else" – a verse from earlier days finds my insisting visiting

The Distance – Then, Now – Ever

I feel, or, perhaps, sense a wisdom,
a knowing in these night hours,
those past the dark rose of midnight.
My thought is not strange to my larger awareness,
together through fullest senses and perceiving,
but I wait, or so the moments pause,
so that I grasp their necessary treasure.
Most, I feel an aloneness, an inability to speak,
as if the gentle muse had left my shoulder –
and oh, the shadow I so manifest,
without her constant offerings of word-blossoms,
I know the world has journeyed into the winter of my life,
to slowly come inside of me,
to consume and disassociate my heart from my
thought and senses as they have been
ever with me,
reason to be at variance with sentiment
inside their mutual chambre.
"Must and can":
my now most recent, truest utterance –
alongside a myriad of souls who have so processed,
and so thought – I will begin again,
to come, again, the distance I have come,
it to be the final portion
of the reaching, the clasping –
the sweet revenge in triumph of the thought, taken –
"..the last of life, for which the first was made."

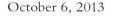

October 6, 2013
two-twenty am
in waking, reaching to find my book of verse,
that reading just before dropping off to sleep,
to read more of new day, somehow thinking the verse to be,
now, that of another writer; familiarity pressed,
however, in truth –
the partial line of poetry quoted, as the last line of my verse,
is taken from Robert Browning's verse "Rabbi Ben Ezra."

With Unattending

The sadness, with its sensation of heaviness,
its aura of dark and ominous portendings –
I am bent, bent so that I grieve into myself when
the image of the stalwart pine comes before my inward eye.
I cannot say the reasoning which is accompaniment
to my grief, only that it has been within,
and always where laughter and youthful joy
most often reign with their happy reminders of self
and its forward movements.
Insults, whether of speaking or of some metaphorical
striking, exact their full exchange in these moments.
In the setting of these exacting, I could not fully respond,
but gathered all into myself, to portion the hurt;
however, all has become a mound of unexpressed grief
with no losing of it, in any effective fashioning.
The blossom bends in the unforgiving warmth as the cheek
pales under the ravaging of time –
and I am spent with effort at either defending
or denying, to lie upon my bed, a wasted vessel of glory –
the dressing of freedom,
the arranging of a worthy fulfillment.
I am lost into the forgetfulness of an assemblage
of friend and kin, a work, purpose, and
the full journey of becoming.
These all looked and did not see,
did not come to touch, yet afford glances to one
whose heart has come to be a castaway,
feeling the power of the dress of difference,
the dragon of withholding of nourishment
in utterance and acceptance.

Unattended roses and creekside violets –
beauty that can flourish alone, under the only eye of God;
but the godman, his very gifted heart, must need, at some times,
to go home to recognition, acknowledgment, acceptance –
else celestial or terrestrial – or its flowering
will perish in its unattending.

December, 2013
in deepest night

difficult to say (script), but an honest
expression of some moments –

On Beauty

"Beauty is, as beauty does."
There is no fatigue, greater, than that of the press
of hours alone, when one is unhappy with his self –
a self that feels unable, unattractive, but, most,
unloved; it stands, then, a significant principle,
that we be responsive, to more, at times, but, certainly,
at times, to less.
We are said to be "blessed" if we can be alert to our
environment, especially through giving, caring,
being thoughtful into knowing,
and industrious, yet loving,
in all of its many faces.
Complimenting the love activity, sometimes,
and often, is the activity of creating:
bringing beauty into existence when it is not present,
or refashioning, adding to, and such.
This activity brings communication,
and the self is made content, and therefore,
more pleasing,
evoking warmth for beautiful fulfilling,
through others.

The circle, then can be happily drawn.

May 10, 2013
in deepest night
heavy rain, falling –

Second Lament

A song does bleed forth
the blush of my heart,
flowing out from within its deep,
my crimson passion, yet a wounding;
how can morning's empowering splendor manifest,
yet, again, and how will the dew fall
effervescing into its heavens, bringing fullest day –
how –
for, oh God, spent are my dreams,
my precious dreams –
unrealized treasure – my little babes of thought and idea,
of intention and movement –
now, now –
in their being, in their absence, their only
premonition ed, ever, to be.

December 20, 2013
in deepest night, toward morning, one–fify am
having read a verse from 2010 (*Seasonal Portions*)
at this time of the closing of the year, regarding my dreams –
another time, escaping capture –

Life is ever the same, our reach exceeding our grasp,
ever, still, very piercing to my heart.

The suggested phrase...our reach should exceed our grasp...is
from R. Browning's verse "Andrea del Sarto"

Not Presently

The feast is not, presently, calling me to table;
finally, I know that the year, before it began,
in its flowing, it increases even more,
and has, always, been difficult;
I am together only by a recipe of three components
coming into place: a large covering
of apathy (a distance with all things);
denial, and turning inward, all conflict.
Such an approach to overpowering conflict and
accumulative fatigue leaves the feast wounded,
and inappropriate – or perhaps,
a fable I have constructed.
Yet, memory of its hours in glory sadden me,
"et je pleure."

December 15, 2013
in deepest night
"Joy cometh in the morning," but it is still, now, night,
in its "forever."

Victorious, and Lost

And when the help is finished,
and the day closes,
sleep is a welcome friend – no questions,
or requirements, quite like its lorded self -
the great sleep, giving every balm to every wound,
without the tease of waking.
So small our universes become, the dark before,
and into the dark, and with a reticence to granting,
accepting memory of light, the glory,
the victory into lostness –
victoriously lost.
To reason so is to a relief, if an abomination,
but, then, why not the full wager -
I am weary, weary with being,
weary in questioning:
how many times must I die.

January 19, 2013
nine o'clock pm

saying through scripting – since there is not ever audience -
such exorcises the sentiment, offering relief of tension -
at least until the next time -
being eventually aware is a victory some of us seek -
only to know the fuller reality of loss in it:
a point from which there are reprieves granted,
but no full return permitted -

Andso, tell me, again, the fable of Job – will,
of whatever complextion – doomed –
all we need is to accept, to be, then, victorious, and lost -

The Gentle Suggestion

Returning quickly to my bed,
I lifted the crimsoned, flesh-colored blankets,
to feel my body's warmth was still in them:
the closeted flame, my own fire, my passion –
my just now resting soul –
and in that moment, with an immediacy,
sensing life, vibrant, true –
I almost knelt, and did weep, that I knew,
was advised softly, if metaphorically,
that I did live, in joy with bitter –
but that I did live, and that I was, at table,
in the feast.

January 27, 2013
in deepest night
about two-thirty am – peace –

To the First of Day

I opened my lips to speak,
crimsons and rouge against ivory touwle, resting;
and there sounded, in these beauty,
the finding of humanity's heavy, waiting stance:
words of prophetic beginnings:
"Mamma, Mamma."
To such my heart knew a pregnant sigh,
emitting cries carrying prefacing wisdom,
couched in eons' clasp, to gather back truths
of hearth and song, a yearning berceuse –
again found to the first of day, open crimsons,
closing in deference to this telling, spoken moment.

April 29, 2013
upon waking, near six o'clock, am
dawn, now – the impatient visitor –

I recognize, in these lines, my singularly complete,
no one to receive my thought, its words –
only I to hear my own conscious awareness –
I was in heavy warmth, and I was cold –
a kind of patience forcing into a fashion of
commanding nature – my bells in familiar accompaniment –

I am not afraid, but near the pain in fragmentation;
I must to somehow act, to put in place.

Smiles

If the fig can smile its morning rose,
and the moon her iridescent pearl;
the pine, its emeraled, overpowering gaze,
its full strength above all below –
then I will gently show two morning – glories
above apple and cherry, placed just so on softest,
silken ivory –
these, in my springtime, haloed raven, about,
now with the silver of winter's first snowfall.
The premier artist, the absolute author of good,
finds representative hues in nature's full repertoire,
its issuance already out His complete,
that gentle and fierce; and from this larder He traverses
the world of energy, to, with an elixir of love,
draw only the beautiful,
in each and all,
these hues His true ambassadors,
emitting the faces of the God-head,
to shapen and fragrance into fullest rapture,
finally through transposing sounds –
these, his temples, to be kept by reason,
tempered by mercy, aside, ever,
from Adam's judgment.

September 21, 2013
evening time, resting, with thoughts –

The Full of September

Soundings of my geese in the south woods;
coming darkness reminding moonglow;
wheels quietening into familiar solitude,
thought returning to careful unknowing –

It is just now the evenfall,
and I am gifted a day, spilled over compari,
passed into that great, cathedraled hall of hours,
yesterday; shadows play off remaining light,
and night winds are finding place –
more the ambiance is one of greater softness,
since the calendar has shown September –
beauty of newest finding against beauty in a first lostness,
the elixir, a moment of reflection.
The full wash of gold has not yet arrived,
but it is, in every turn of the faithful lock,
in expectancy; spent with the vibrancy
of daily radiance that fills summer hours,
the coquette, a semblance of twilight chill,
conjures up lovely scenes decorated in Maple red,
Goldenrod, harvest wealth, and, waiting to come
to the fore, umbers out the earth,
punctuated by burnt and bright sienna.
The cataloging passed hurriedly among my thoughts,
and I was, together, bewildered at my discovery of the
approaching hour of the year's
"last, loveliest smile."
Included in this discovery – not at all its first –
echoed a statement out past questioning and frustration:
"Why...everything that should bring happiness
to you brings unhappiness."

The loveliness of the early evening already was calling
out a familiar despondency, and the accusing statement –
somehow, in all my risings up, and lyings down –
had finally savored my whole self so that I
could know a principle which spoke my centras:
my life is, has been, always, and will continue,
a bitter sweetness, a September, an autumn –
in thought and behavior, a looking backward,
and forward, to conclusion.
Beauty, the morning to every day,
whatever its fashioning,
is only for a season, and must be lost,
to be recaptured, over, and again,
lest I faint within the twines of the limberlost,
to seek out the flame,
a perceived ultimate in the all beautiful.
Can my dalliance in despair be more than is –
or must I, as he with the stone and the mountain,
over, and over again –
enter the only adventure, leaving the provided circumstance:
ever September, ever the confection
of passing beauty, ever the accepted – raptured –
ever the waiting into perishing –
the only, ever – the existential-
the bitter sweet.

September 8, 2013
thoughts while resting, waiting nightfall, following a lovely
afternoon, with delightful images of the day past –

What Finding

Where did the day go -
just, then, with the smile of sunlight,
growing into its moments -
Is the day nestled behind a wish,
a question, or perhaps, resting in a
velvet box with memory
and sentimental hymns
to the glory of past moments.
How to find the sunlight,
the smile that is most true to our being -
the exclamation to all thought, rising,
to continuance, beside delight -
what finding is more treasure.

August 11, 2013
Mamma's or Daddy's birthday – one or the other -
the remaining, August 14 -
a comment on the surreal quality of a great number of my "days"-
into the recency of unheard music, softly heard,
in fullest hearing, yet – continuing, with beauty -

Review

In soft climes of coming matron years,
glory was accounted once and again,
to surprise and care, fulfilled expectations,
and admiration touched by a hesitant,
if kind respect.
But the long, grey halls, those of heavy steps,
and solitude – these, without awareness,
yet as they moved between "glories" –
those very nearly took away deepest spirit,
and did, in hours quiet escaping ordinary description, bend –
for joy in the feast of day often came only in
a glimpse of light, it falling on the revered
rose of rose, of early hearth hours.
And in quiet moments – those away from routine and necessity,
familiar bells would become gentle,
and noble thought fell a full drape over spreaded sorrow.
Perhaps the inside of worthy thought,
its purity and loveliness, should must to be kept –
secret to the heart –
to be found only through scripting,
and that intuited by fellows of strong rapport.
And then, the coming together of the felt, sensing word,
and its found knowing – it to be surely understood –
yes then, please, then – poets will, in company,
sound the beauty of worded thought.
The night, then, would not ever fall,
as not a season enters, having, formerly this entrance,
here, as familiar, eager scapes, yet an eon
approaching from silent waiting;
and in glory would beauty stand –
most in worthy light – the strength of mortal will,
having drunk a fine nectar of honey mead –
the draught of we "lesser gods" –
of the divine, manifest.

June 8, 2013
anniversary to Daddy's death, twenty-three years
Roman thoughts hovering close by — with angst in the
assessment of my years —

Not Anymore in Struggle

Of my self I sing, again, once more,
that the tension of my heart's knowings
be exorcised into the beauty of Presence,
that inside the cosmos of Its
rainbow hued imaginings.
I wish love and understanding – and tolerance,
which is the great manifestation of good –
let these lie over all as the gentle coverlet
of parental care – beautiful, warm, and, in its full
flowering, only all of good.

November 27, 2013
once more, thinking of Thanksgiving Day

I am alone, but I am not in struggle, for Holy Presence has
visited me this year, since the great wounding of the holiday
period of las year. I fear less, and my yearnings, my longings –
these lie in patience – somewhere, some somewhere, at a distance;
I almost weep at the loss, or, perhaps better said, "placing,"
of my passionate intensities which have always, in sum,
taken my joy. Today, the "feast" overshadows the combined losses
I have known, and I am, in the moment,
content. Thanks be to God.

November 28, 2013
Thanksgiving Day

In these true comments, I am flirting with
depersonalization, but I am
no longer fearful of that which I am ill, and
that with which I have had the
help of celestial, and terrestrial resources, nearly bested.

And I wrote into the night – I am love to
no one – the only conclusion,
for it is the conclusion – of all – but, yet -
"black is the color of my true love's hair" -
truly do not remember –

Summer White Gold

Becoming a mood almost with eerie foreboding,
was the sudden awareness of true summer sunlight –
always in early July, in Mississippi.
Like a familiar geister, however,
it appears to conscious thought,
at least to some, not a wholly threatening presence,
but with the attributes of familiarity,
and associations, pleasant.
Within sunlight, an abundance of good is easily apparent – lovely,
hanging blossoms, long twilights, fields of cotton,
the great good of ripe fruit – beside picnics, church revivals,
and long visits with relatives.
But known in the sudden awareness, is the immediate
observation that the foreboding is true,
that dark secrets lie in the shadows,
if partially metaphorical.
In these realized moments,
the sun dons a white gold presence, and its entourage
includes a glaring, full sun emptiness,
accompanied by still, silent mirages:
water appearing as mirrors on unforgiving – fiery –
soiled pavement; lost articles from passers-by,
scattered about like lonely wanderers; refreshing,
night rainfall remaining as spider-webbing in small collections,
and petals falling, into wilting dry, reminding.
Heat is so that a raw cleavage seems likely,
even appropriate in various gapings about –
red, raw and burning flesh into scabbing decay,
quivering inside odors that embellish such realities.

There is no escaping the white gold,
for it has the qualities of reforming, finding, oppressing –
these not departing other than in the respite of night –
not until all of the good is used,
its strength taken by that of still another season.
Perhaps more than physical sustenance is housed
in the grande natural; many other gifts
can find their places, but the wisdom of the July sun,
its white gold presence,
can taunt with its full knowing.
Beauty sustains, yet, its condiments of imaged,
necessary pain, conclusions and unknowing
remain unhappy visitations –
to those, all of us, we, in our local color,
we among the "lesser gods."

July 4, 2013
images collecting for several days –
re-evaluated, and expanded –
made more complete, and clear

Within the Surreal:
the inside reality

Inside the night, when light pales its watch,
we can see ourselves, a glimpse may be,
more clearly, somehow, from peering withal
the darkened maelstrom of self;
all before shouts into the murmuring of yesterday,
the clever manipulations of martyr into monastic;
but all, still, within the ambiance of the fallen,
winged and haloed great, who, as with his many own,
through long, autumnal decent, found his bested, incontent.
How goes the wager – to "glory in the glory," seen,
or else stand consumed in the very poverties of self.
In truest noblesse, perhaps lies the wish to bind,
and not to burke all lesser finds, which only
stand the created now, wrapping robes that do
flow out in natural beauty,
the effort, very wrenched from one's first knowing,
toward the fatigue, the wait of yesterday -
before appetite, presence – and immortal yearnings:
full nativity to travailing day -
and the tendered loss, all inside it.

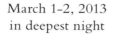

March 1-2, 2013
in deepest night
My many recalled images, in waking, in deepest night, a
mourning, surely of many, and more, exchanges of the day, passed.
Millie, her apparent gentleness, but "innocent" recounting of
"old" John, my "now" John, his intense wish to help my poor
wretchedness, those aimlessly "making the day, in an institution
of lauded mercy, quite genuine to me, on another day –
What, indeed, poor gardens we "cultivate," our walk,
blindly, blithely into the next frame, conversation of it,
quite of the weather – my insight, perhaps of\from my own
inadequacies (ever malaise), bent me, and I poured myself
into my seasoned bed, to lie, lost in the coward's death
(of sleep), gladly giving "my kingdom for a horse" –

explanation\regrets –

Reminder

-faint, but a grande reminder,
through breakfast windows, at table –
ever promising –
a small bouquet of "left-over" blossoms
whose beauty must:
the Gardenia, of fragrance,
even unto loss in recollection;
the Calla lily, in white purity, regal,
of drawing, masterful;
the Rose of rose,
and sentiment that touches from first
hours at the hearth, and the gentle,
somewhat deferring Chrysanthemum,
dressed in a quiet lavender,
speaking conclusion, out of season,
against beginning summer radiance –

June 12, 2013
on sitting down to breakfast, looking out to beginning day,
greeted by my "left-over" bouquet –
what of objective reality – arrangements and such –
beauty know few conclusions –
a fragment: five am

Lines –

In abject silence, my heart has bled crimson,
in beautiful communion with the dark earth, below;
in grandest solitude have the ponderings
inside my thought crushed the light that I,
at all, once saw and felt, to know.

...."comforting lines," continued –

In my hand rests, all of nothing, and my mother's arm
cannot offer, anymore, its comforting bend.
There is, then, nothing to hold, nor any
strong tenderness to bind into – and I am left
the innocent, though weathered, waif – whose steps wander
out beyond safe portals, into the earth of such hued
wounding that nightingales' strewed roses,
of rouge and bright, can no longer be thought.

November 25, 2013
in deepest night
– a sentiment which "just came" at bedtime, on Monday evening,
before Thanksgiving Day

No voice or touch, of any thee –
in darkest, heavy rainfall, yet thousands
of bells, in audible soundings –
-having seen Dr. Norton, earlier in the day,

The hours have become still, carried
across these difficult moments,
the rainfall softening, and thunder, heard
in the far distance – a bramble of
sentiment, the hours carrying memory alongside a cruel reality,
a playing out of a coy tease; the beauty of
festivals, past, are more the disappearing:
butter pates on bread, first berries of summer's radiance –
these having lost firmness – and color.
Light, a generous comma, somewhat,
now, "lazy," slothful in touch.
Yet, a good bathing of rainfall brings images of paintings,
waiting, glimpses of returning hunters,
the unicorn of sweetest legend, all recipes to enjoy a supremacy.

–always in winter and the chill becomes a companion,
with warm beverages, the moment's delight.
Still the tease is most the dragon of knowing –
and we spar in uncommon confusion, it wrapped about by
the beautiful traditional.

Angelic royalty, drawing the moment's finding,
the hearth and fire breathing all content –
ah, these condiments to festival hours
bring longing in distant days.
November 25-26, 2013
in deepest night
a fanciful wandering throughout the night, waking to the true
of Literature and life.

The wealth of peace and joy,
ill-fated to some while blessing to all –
world of worlds enclosed in mystery,
wonder, and simple truth.

–the serpentine curling of the events in time –
record of that past, with no indication of the future –

and the morning came –

Continuation... "New Lines..."

— preserving thought by preserving the body –
gradual until final loss,
and then significance and "making it," adjustively –

August 25, 2014

The seasons preface themselves through
various patterns of winds and sunlight,
flora and temperature,
a relaxing of the intensity of summer's radiance,
a confection of dubious sweetness.

Final weeks of August, 2014

The quiet, and its full ambiance
gave up words and thought.

"Right" is overly complicated;
"wrong" is deceitful.

August 26, 2014

October, Deep Night Fragment

When the moon is down,
and the hour is great,
giester appear in white, alert to the company
Of thrashing souls,
but sporting in active contemplation of truth.
The style, the fashioning of stillness
Follow on the stage of the objective worlds,
these located with the essence of moonlight
attending the subjective self.

October 28, 2013
near midnight
on waking this morning, I found these words, poorly
scripted, incomplete, on my writing pad; they comprise
a partial fragment – of an idea, an image I understood
when the words were written – but sleep is a clever pirate,
taking, without consideration, of circumstance

Restatement

Slowly, but eagerly entering the marvel of early day,
Finds it fresh and promising,
Despite its passing out is companion,
The dying night,
Whose dirge arranged as the day's
Moments in singularity – dark and grey wanderings.
Metaphorically, words scripted,
Lift out truths nature imepts, and yet, and still,
The energies of the self,
If ever in wellness,
Pushes past these realizations to the gold,
The silver and diamonds, worthy brass,
And splendid copper –
The wealth of prologued experience –
Such then – these filling hands, clasping, with a will,
Before the balm is graciously past,
Searching out knowing –
The grail, everward.

Beauty, as it grows, in ever daily, now –
and falls a shadow, over raw reality,
knowing what not to put aside,
transmuting all into itself, if for a season;
let wander, us all, long into the blest,
out dews, into our most selves – dark into light, this passing –
again, Sarto, a "balance," struck.

July 27, 2013

Aura Victory

Words carry, around them, definings,
each an aura —
"butterfly": glows freedom, joy, in beauty;
anniversary and birthday evenings: flow through
the magic of the night;
and returning steps: the music of gratitude singing the
absolute glory of the completed day.
We cannot hold all that comes to be ours,
either that seen, touched, or felt but
through the power of thought,
a wisdom can work its work so that
there is memory, through metaphor, symbol, repetition —
in reason and thought,
whose transport we cannot fully explain,
these coming into deep sentiment.
A swelling of the hurt, or joy, like a string of the lyre,
wind rushing through as fingers adroit and masterful.
Oh my soul, forgive my emptiness,
come of my own to be my own;
let the sloth arrived out puny injuries
become aware of its smallness,
that of its stings, and, to the side, the hurting blows.
Work gratefulness about our chagrin,
and make whole with the joy of being.

July 25, 2015
One o'clock am
– after a day of disappointments, and unknown insults –
until the quiet opened them for observation and evaluation –
coming, however, the realization that such, in its
whole, is just "wine over the shoulder: –

August Epiphany

Tense, specific (static) or in flow,
Is in every moment,
And that of arriving, "being," is\will always be "now":
And, if living in true wholeness –
A moment of acute realization,
Moments of full awareness;
And times of pause, of still, do occur,
But are truly only reducing of the movement,
A re-arranging of the flow, not an emptiness,
A nothingness, not that fatally conclusive.
We need know this principle, else our breath,
Our voice of life,
Never be heard in its fullness –
Felt – experienced as the cessation of a lover's longing.
This sense of urgency is not a complex,
Of covering, of fugue, or displacement,
But eager, joyful grasping:
Ah, to reach, Mr. Browning!

August 20, 2015
Breakfasting early, content, thoughtful
Six-thirty am

The reference to "Mr. Browning," is to the famed
English Victorian poet, and his very well-known line
from the verse, "Andrea del Sarto,": "Ah, but a man's
reach should exceed his gasp, or what's a heaven for."

It Is Easier Now...

It is easier, in now recent times, to ask forgiveness of God (Holy Presence) than either person or circumstance; particulars in the realm of the social rather than the traditional simply demand more conscious strength and will, being more concrete, rather than abstract – an evolving backward, seemingly, but quite obviously.

But we have been taught scenes, trends, and then rules, laws and such that there is a faint remembrance that God is, at the final, merciful, kind, forgiving, and we take the best of both worlds – but so – God is also, at least, reasonable – and most, balanced, as the universe suggests – ancient, (having once been) sayings – from where or how, unimportantly – but certain in their reality – lean toward this hypothesis. And so we do not ever rest – only in the complete state of equity – death – and then we are certain only in surmise.

We are pitiable creatures with enough knowing to dream the dream of peace ("sweetness and light"), but to find it – the long wait of individual faith, inward to the nothing of our beautiful, if cruel, humanity – but rather in the bountiful spirit – lovely fulfilling – acknowledged – aware repose – unthinkable to us "lesser gods."

Most, we follow seasons, cycles, routines, and schedules, they erupting periodically, consciously or no, by wish or circumstance – only to return to a pre-experienced model, until we must "break out" again, having learned little from former outings: individuals, groups, cities, states, countries – these happenings often finding their impetus in the classroom, the visitor from "afar," natural disasters, and movements cloistered inside certain breasts of thought.

We are creatures who have and know patterns, full and good but must to risk "cutting out," even if anything new is chaos and confusion – the joy, the energy, the grail – to build again.

–the ever saga: passion and resting –

October 6, 2015
a prose verse

Part Songs

These are "part songs" of verses that somehow became
separated from their wholes; the dates are present,
without the entire verse. I have lifted out of these (what
of them I now have) some of the better voicings.

June 2, 2016

Thoughts, deep into the night, each leading to fundamental
constructs in the understanding of the grey, and sometimes bright
"openings," in the path (roads) of life.
The conclusion is one being worked toward,
out great dissonance – fire and passion, of
necessity, of examination, full.
I can know, with the breathlessness of Dante under his stars,
to finally accept that given,
except the fashioning of my stance chosen, in it.
Harpies are still realities to us mortals, but grief prepares content,
and, then, there is the "balance," of "walking
these golden, earthly sands.

–"Walking these...earthly sands." – The refrain for a
verse to my mother, my child, my sister, my friend –
years ago on "Mother's Day," following her death –

- recognition, and the realization of the
must rearranging of passion,
these in deliverance toward quiet and gently known content.
beautiful, then, is to visit at table, to, in narratives, sweet,
know the troth, past description, of thought and sentiment,
in which the days of the sunken pomegranate's
cheeks are worded into coming to be;
a joining saga, a metamorphose in that of delicious,
adventuresome rebellion, these into tears,
and Samaritan bindings out the armored heart;
advancing, still, philosophical joustings come
to smile at doubt and questioning, into a meadow of stillness,
dressed in silence, these varietal principles coming to be put aside,
not in denial or impotence, but in truth of mortal unveiling,
a final crown to us "lesser gods."

Then, oh then – a balance strikes, the heart becoming tender
In its constricted heaviness.
This magic lies in every morning, the hours flowing love,
If individually experienced.
The fuller histoire finds all –
The thief, the leper, the courtesan; the savior,
Kings and serfs, yet the cynic, the cleric, and the warrior.

- Tomorrow – the clock is still, to reason,
the attire of the players in full fluidity.
And the movement is all of time.
There is no anemic answer, to her consort,
The unfounded question; the wine and the grape are one;
All is in the moment's flow, and,
In the moment, is all of time.
November 5, 2013

What love, loveliness,
come to me — is any in my readers;
I am alone —
slowly, the eventuality —
slower, than the reality —

Could I have been, in some other universe,
some other sense of self —
some fields of a Carthage — somehow existent —
so that I knew this beauty, always, completely,
for which I now, in quite different climes, yearn,
in a kind of pain, a mourning —
that I, as Persepernie, be allowed to travel back to earth
(somewhere), again, if for a short while,
but with certainty, every new year.

— Does death to life, or death in life —
separate us from peace,
this question answered, individually:
a true pathos of we "lesser gods."

The chosen steps of all loves are seasons to finality —
in eventide, which falls with the twilight,
recognizing the fullness of the day,
to beautiful, sweetest pain,
the careful acknowledgment of conclusion.

The hour is approaching three – thirty am as I conclude this verse; it is commemorative to the every spring I experience, or have experienced, since early childhood. The circumstance is always similar: I mourn, I grieve the passing of such great beauty, a truth I realized very early. I became ill in the spring, near Easter, and I am not fully certain that I will be, ever, entirely separate from these experiences. Time is a strange circumstance to me; I do not feel that I can be comfortable, conclusively, with its passing. My pieces will always be my "working through" a very severe construct – perhaps allowing me, all the more adept, then, at dealing with the very "passing" away of our truest selves.

These words, embracing, scripting may tortured thought –
we, and mine, speak often of everything, and nothing –
never referencing my name –
only work, coming seasons, families, restaurants –
recent tragedies, travel, the ever political saga –
anything – everything but the poor reading of my recounting.
Andso, I retire to my rooms, and pleasure myself
amid symptomatic anhedonia.

elizabeth afterthought
To "Thoughts in Deepest Night"

-a chariot, a sound, new fallen rain to quieten old hurt;
a touch, a remembered image of sweetest sentiment –

The Basket

My beauty, and spirited step, into the away,
Quieting friendships, with movement –
Family, wandered, somehow –
Now almost at the distance of the horizon;
Love, among its beautiful ruins;
Memory, a companion, sweet –
These, if left the help, inside a waiting basket –
These shadowed jewels –
These would be left me, if choice be made.

Thoughts ...

How to bear knowing, and
feeling the knowing;
we look about, review our strengths,
and sadly understand that we will not
die, but will engage all of it in full
cognizance, after some fashion,
not yet to surmise even the medium
open to us.

Elizabeth
several days before
Christmas, 2015

Thoughts....

The Marvelous of Perception

There is loss in all,
but findings in every other,
yet more wealth in that taken.
If this principle can be accepted,
summer will arrive, in fullest radiance,
no matter the long of winter's grey.
Friendship with pain, then, is route to peace
by the steps of discipline,
fancy of what might be;
and the grande indulgence of what good,
what beauty – the brilliance of purity –
these are glory of time passed.

April 16, 2013
on waking, just past six o'clock am

how marvelous the properties of the perceptive process –
therefore, the bright of first butterflies,
grace in strongest, tender burking's of
Morning Glory's climbing tendrils –

the finding in silenced thought,
a selective stance with every sensation,
the rest in struggle of all existence –

we find in visitations that which we bring –